DATE DUE

OCT - 7 2001	

BRODART, INC.   Cat. No. 23-221

Assumptions of Social Psychology
A Reexamination

Assumptions of Social Psychology
A Reexamination

Robert E. Lana
Temple University

LEA LAWRENCE ERLBAUM ASSOCIATES, PUBLISHERS
1991   Hillsdale, New Jersey   Hove and London

Lawrence Erlbaum Associates, Inc., Publishers
365 Broadway
Hillsdale, New Jersey 07642

Library of Congress Cataloging-in-Publication Data

Lana, Robert E., 1932-
   Assumptions of social psychology : a reexamination / Robert E.
Lana.
      p.   cm.
   Includes bibliographical references and indexes.
   ISBN 0-8058-1022-6. — ISBN 0-8058-1023-4
   1. Social psychology.   I. Title
HM251.L242   1991
302 — dc20   91-6637
                                                             CIP

Printed in the United States of America
10 9 8 7 6 5 4 3 2 1

Contents

Preface

Biologists, physicists, and chemists have clearly demonstrated their ability to accumulate an ever-increasing store of information that convinces all that their respective fields progress in an orderly fashion. Even accepting that theoretical and methodological paradigmatic shifts have occurred, progress in the natural sciences is palpable although the social consequences of such progress are often problematic. Such is not the case with social psychology.

Why has social psychology not shown the same empirical and theoretical advancement as the natural sciences over the past 40 years? I believe that this is a reasonable question to ask today, and one that we, in part, have the answer to.

It has been 20 years since *Assumptions of Social Psychology* was published and social psychology has changed mightily in that time in well-documented fashion. The questions about the empirical and epistemological quality of the field raised in that book were akin to the more boldly phrased questions above. During the 20 years that have passed, social psychologists have gone through, and partially solved, their "crisis," and have become increasingly more sophisticated about the possibilities and limitations of their endeavors. This version of *Assumptions* is my own account of what has happened to the epistemology of social psychology during the past 20 years, and where I believe we find ourselves today.

Imbedded in the comparison of the success of social psychology with the success of the natural sciences in both predicting phenomena and ordering it into theoretically coherent structures, is the question of, if or how social psychology can be an experimental science. This is an issue that has been addressed many times during the past 20 years, and

I would like to summarize my position on that crucial issue. In order to accomplish this task, I believe it is necessary to review certain historical developments, such as Vico's reaction to Descartes regarding the social basis of rationality, as well as reviewing the idea of causation as set forth in the Hume–Kant contributions of the 18th century.

A major thesis is that the epistemologies utilized by social scientists encompassing behavioral, cognitive, and historical analyses are complimentary rather than contradictory. In order to demonstrate this, the historical underpinnings of social psychological epistemologies and an argument for the complimentarity of major social psychological theoretical approaches are developed. Most importantly, some of the possibilities for building explanation of social phenomena, which are alternatives to existing forms of explanation, are discussed.

This book is dedicated to the future generation and especially to Renata Lana, and to the present generation and especially to Ralph Rosnow, and to the memory of Marianthi Georgoudi.

Robert E. Lana

CHAPTER 1

Introduction

It is difficult to resist comparing progress in social psychological explanation with that in the natural sciences. Few social psychologists would agree that their work has resulted in the same accumulation of predictive successes and coherent theory as has occurred in fields such as physics, chemistry, or biology. As for comparing the success of social psychology with other subfields of psychology such as personality, behavior theory, or developmental psychology, they are all so integrally related that the result may not be worth the effort.

There are at least two levels at which dissatisfaction with the pace of progress in social psychology has occurred during the years since World War II. At the empirical level, methodological issues of the sort contained under the rubric of artifacts in experimental design is one such set of problems, and the place of the experiment itself as the principal tool in developing social psychological theory is the principle problem at the epistemological level. Both levels are addressed throughout the course of this book.

There has always been a controversy surrounding the use of objective methods, particularly the scientific experiment, in answering questions about complex human processes such as social interaction and, in the past, consciousness itself, however defined (e.g., James, 1962; Lashley, 1923). As early as 1890 William James was wary of the use of experiments to explain complex human behavior. He believed that the deterministic assumption, best served by experimental analysis, is merely provisional and methodological and that the assumption of determinism is therefore open to discussion on a level other than the scientific. He understood that a psychologist who wishes to build a science must at least tacitly take the deterministic position. However, the psychologist does not, therefore, have to believe that all human characteristics are explainable by deterministic, scientific methods.

John Watson's (1913) shift in emphasis from the study of the contents of consciousness to the study of behavior, championed direct observation over the previous dependence on introspection practiced by 19th-century psychologists. Watson, against the study of consciousness per se, developed his argument against the validity of introspection as the principal method of psychology. The introspective analysis of consciousness had yielded a great deal of controversy. The laboratories of different investigators produced different conclusions about the same phenomenon depending on the theoretical bias of the psychologist. Discrepancies were essentially uncheckable because they depended on the introspection of the trained observers of each of the laboratories. There was no agreed upon basis by which hypotheses could be tested.

Watson's idea that behavior had to be the data of psychology required the additional assumption that the sense data of the observer of behavior was the key element in the process. What the observer could see, hear, smell, and so forth, could be confirmed by another observer and consensus could easily be reached regarding the nature of the data under examination. This, in turn, meant that the controlled experiment could become the principal method of the behaviorist. Watson was careful to indicate that this approach did not eliminate the fact of either the presence or absence of consciousness, which was, by definition, unobservable.

Karl Lashley (1923), working 10 years after Watson's position was initially published, held that science, defined as the examination of sense data via an objective method such as the experiment, is not appropriate for an examination of felt experience and, therefore, of consciousness. Later, Lashley, Tolman (1927), and Hull (1943), although not denying its existence, were also to exclude consciousness from the possibility of fruitful examination by the methods of science.

Despite those reservations concerning the use of experiment to answer questions about complicated human functions by some of the leading psychologists of the early part of the century, Carl Iver Hovland and his associates (Hovland, Janis, & Kelley, 1953; Hovland, Lumsdaine, & Sheffield, 1949) launched postwar experimental social psychology with his persuasion experiments while gathering about him many disciples who were to become the country's leading exponents of experiment applied to social problems. From 1945 until the mid-1960s, we worked diligently on discovering the details of how people formed and changed their attitudes, beliefs, and opinions, and how, or if, behavior followed, and how it could be changed in a good cause. It became clear during the 1960s that many conclusions could not be supported by research from other laboratories or from our own replication. The study of attitudes, beliefs, opinions, and the persuasive process then experienced the same reduction of generalizability of results and the accompanying narrowing of experimental focus that other experimental efforts (e.g., those of Clark L. Hull) suffered in the late 1940s. It was in the 1960s that a number of social psychological experimenters began discovering crucial difficulties in their experimental procedures. These difficulties were not of the usual variety, involving calibrations of various kinds or changes in procedure in order to better elicit a response from the subject. Rather, social psychologists discovered that the subject entered into the experimental procedure in a way that had not been expected. In an experiment, variation in the subject is either controlled directly by the experimenter by manipulation of the relevant independent variables or is presumed to vary randomly over a number of subjects. Difficulty arose when some of those uncontrolled variables that were thought to vary randomly, were responses from the subject directed toward being in the experiment itself. In short, by interpreting various aspects of his or her participation in an experiment, the subject introduced a confounding variable that rendered the results of the study either meaningless or grossly distorted. Sufficient interest in these distorting variables was generated to produce a body of research on artifacts in social psychological experimentation. This research was summarized and discussed by a number of involved social psychologists in Robert Rosenthal and Ralph Rosnow's now well-known *Artifact in Behavioral Research,* which appeared in 1969. The suspiciousness of the subject of the experimenter's intent, whether or not a subject had volunteered to appear in a study, whether or not a pretest was used to evaluate some characteristic of the subject before an experimental treatment was applied, what the subject believes is required of him or her in an experiment, what the subject believes the experimenter expects of him, and whether the subject is anxious about participating in an experiment, all appeared as factors that could distort the meaning of the experimental results. In the decade of the 1970s, research continued on artifacts in the experimental process, further refining the nature of the difficulties more often than eliminating them. Since the late 1960s, social psychologists have had a choice; they could continue to perform experiments in order to eventually minimize or eliminate the effects of unwanted subject influence in the social psychological experiment, or they could concentrate on the very nature of the experiment itself and its place in a field that purported to discover information on the nature of social existence. One could also, of course, do both, but with separate efforts. This crisis in social psychology has been well documented (e.g., Rosnow, 1981) and we need not deal with it here. What I prefer to focus on is the progress that has been made in the field since the late 1960s, progress that has largely taken the two avenues already suggested. In the late 1980s we have become both more empirically astute and epistemologically more sophisticated than we were 20 years ago. Controversy still abounds, but of course it would and should in a field with intelligent, energetic practitioners.

In the 20 years that have elapsed since the first edition of this work, there have not been startlingly new theoretical successes based on experimental research in social psychology compared with success in, for example, biology with its discovery of the DNA molecule. There has been interesting new work in social psychology (e.g., Altman's, 1976, fusion of the physical environment with social arrangements, Nisbett and Ross', 1980, attribution of causality as a social judgment) but the accumulation of useful predictions about social phenomena has not kept pace with the successes of the natural sciences by any means, although there are different rates of success among physics, chemistry, and biology. Assuming social psychologists are as intelligent, resourceful, and creative on the whole as natural scientists, and I have no reason to doubt that they are not, it is imperative that we discover the factors that account for the different rates of success of social psychology compared with those of the natural sciences.

Social psychologists know how to do an experiment. They understand the logic of the process and are as resourceful and creative as any other scientist in designing an empirical test of a hypothesis. I am convinced that our lack of significant progress compared with that of the natural scientists is not based upon technical or logical failures as experimenters. It is based instead on the nature of our defined subject matter and the way we conceive the nature of our problems. The questions we ask and the solutions that are logically and technically feasible need to be carefully delineated. We have been discussing various epistemological aspects of social psychology over the past 20 years. Many of the controversies that have arisen can now be resolved. Many of us will continue to do experiments and others will concentrate on epistemological issues; that is the way it should be in a healthy field. However, one epistemological possibility is that there may be logical limitations to answering certain questions about the nature of the human socius through experimental methods. Other questions can only be answered by experimental analysis. I attempt to separate the two here.

Finally, some explanations, particularly those that seem incomplete, may nevertheless satisfy some people more than others who insist on the apparent finality of the development of a scientific law. What kind of explanation we are satisfied with as social psychologists is also at issue and is discussed in later chapters.

THE EMPIRICAL FOCUS OF THE PAST 20 YEARS

Perhaps the single best record of change and development in social psychological methods and theories since the late 1960s is Lindzey and Aronson's 1985 edition of *The Handbook of Social Psychology*. The two volumes of the handbook contain reviews of the experimental and theoretical efforts of social psychologists in all of the major subareas of the field, thus there is no need for such reviews to be presented here. However, I discuss some of the material regarding attitude to illustrate certain changes in the practice of social psychology.

William McGuire (1985), in his excellent chapter on attitudes and attitude change, has identified certain historical periods where interest ran high in how attitudes change, and what procedures one may use to change them. In the first period, that of Pericles 500 years before the birth of Christ, the art of persuasion was conceived to be the mastering of one or another set of principles of rhetoric. The second period ends with the demise of Cicero in 43 B.C. and again depends on oratorical principles. Rhetoric and hermeneutics were also the subject of 15th- and 16th-century orators who flourished in the liberal period of the Italian Renaissance. McGuire placed the fourth period of intense interest in persuasion and attitudes from the 18th century to the current, with emphasis on the late 19th to 20th centuries as a result of the industrial revolution and its attendant interest in the distribution of large numbers of new goods, and the accompanying changes in customs and social beliefs that inevitably followed.

It is the change in approach between the first, second, and third persuasion eras on the one hand, and the fourth period on the other, which is of central significance to some of the changes that occurred in the empirical and theoretical pursuit of answers to social psychological problems during the past 20 years of our own era. The Greek, Roman, and Italian periods of approach to attitude and persuasion were rhetorical in nature, whereas the modern period beginning in the 18th century and continuing to today, is positivistic in the broadest sense. We see in later chapters that the rhetorical form, under different guise, has been reintroduced into both the lexicon of social psychological theorizing as well as into the conceptual characterization of social psychological problems of all sorts, including those involving attitudes and persuasion. (See chapter 6 on Hermeneutics and Rhetoric.)

Attitude Change and Persuasion

The concept of attitude is so central to many general ideas of social existence that the theories developed to explain how people form attitudes and the applications that are drawn from these theories are reflected in many other theoretical areas within social psychology in particular and psychology in general. This centrality of the concept of attitude, however defined, has been both a focal point for research and theory as well as a target to be attacked by social psychologists on the verge of developing a different paradigm. The assumptions involving theory development or empirical approach that sometimes precedes theory is of particular interest.

Attitude research reflects social psychologist's concern about the informational exchange they may expect from the results of an experiment on an individual's functioning in groups, real or symbolic. Although the original question raised in the mid–1960s concerned the issue of whether experiments on attitudes were of any use whatsoever (Lana, 1969, 1976), the accumulated 20 years of thinking on the matter allows us to frame the problem differently. The question now is, "Under what circumstances and for what purposes may a traditional laboratory experiment be reasonably able to answer our questions about the formation and change of attitudes, and when must we move to field studies, environmental examinations or other forms of *in situ* observations to answer our questions?" In addition, certain questions asked about attitude require concepts more typical of traditional sociology with its concern with institutions, ideological phenomena on a mass scale and, ultimately, the history of a group, than of social psychology.

There is still a mélange of methods accompanying almost as many theories in attitude research now as in 1969. The difference now is that researchers are more aware of the place of their methodology and of their theory within the layers of explanation that are possible for the phenomenon we call *attitude* and all its manifestations. In 1975, Fishbein and Ajzen still speak of the myriad working definitions of attitude that are used by researchers and theorists of various stripes. Clearly no agreement has been reached in defining terms, yet I am convinced that progress of a sort has been made.

If we concentrate for a moment on the apparent inability of social psychologists to agree on a working definition of attitude, we may conclude that the difficulty lies with the complexity of the phenomenon they are examining and with the difficulty of manipulating attitudinal variables by the usual experimental methods. Why is this so? One reason is that the very definition of attitude always refers to an integrated process in the human being, such as disposition to respond in a certain manner to an identifiable class of objects, or McGuire's "responses that locate objects of thought on dimensions of judgment." Integrated processes do not easily lend themselves to conceptual dissection. Whatever the operational or conceptual definition, and literally hundreds have been counted (Fishbein & Ajzen, 1972), consistent predictions of attitude responses over even the same situations have never been found by any researcher. There are always major exceptions. Consistent predictions of specific responses in even restricted situations are hardly ever accomplished. What has been accomplished over the past 20 years is the development of a richer, more sophisticated picture of human decision making when the objects and processes about which decisions are made are social.

N. H. Anderson's (1981) integration theory is one of the more successful attempts both to explain responses attributable to attitudes, and to place attitudes within a broader range of social psychological phenomena. The nature of this success is of critical importance for understanding the quality of explanation in social psychology and its similarities and differences to the natural sciences.

Anderson's contention is that multiple causation is responsible for all thought and behavior. These causal factors result in an integration of information available to the individual from which context he or she makes decisions regarding attitudes and beliefs, and behaviors associated with them. Anderson made an implicit distinction between thought and behavior, an issue to be discussed in its own right later in the book. An attitude can be analyzed by applying algebraic models to the thought that precedes human judgments and decisions.

In summarizing many years of research on impression formation, Anderson demonstrated a certain consistency in these judgments. The parallelism hypothesis that demonstrates this consistency is illustrated in Fig. 1.1. Subjects were asked to describe people labeled "level headed," "unsophisticated," and "ungrateful" by selecting adjectives such as "good," "bold," or "humorless" to describe them.

The parallel curves indicate that there is no significant interaction effect and hence Anderson concludes that an averaging model best describes the subject's behavior. The rating response is linear. That is, each adjective has the same meaning and value regardless of what other adjective it is paired with in personal description. A further implication of the parallelism hypothesis is that the meaning of adjectives used to describe people is constant so far as the value of the adjectives to an observer. Anderson contrasted this conclusion to Asch's (1946), where personal adjectives were assumed to change meaning depending on other adjectives with which they were paired. Anderson pointed out

FIG. 1.1. Anderson's parallel theory data. Judgments of likableness of persons described by pairs of personality-trait adjectives. The observed parallelism supports the averaging model of person perception. (Data after Anderson, 1962. Copyright © 1974.)

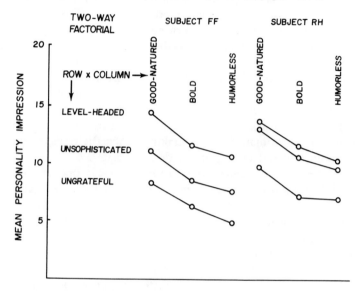

that Asch relied heavily on introspective interpretation on the part of his subjects, and that Asch's results were the products of a semantic illusion dissipated by the experimental results cited previously.

Anderson's careful research over the past 20-odd years is both consistent and impressive. It represents one of the best continuing research programs in contemporary social psychological research. For our purposes, it is useful to contrast Anderson's research process and results with a similar program in one of the traditional natural sciences.

The work by Maurice Wilkins on X-ray diffraction pictures of the DNA molecule that preceded Crick and Watson's (Watson, 1968) model building of its structure, is one of the most significant scientific developments of the 20th century. The biochemical experiments that it spawned changed the nature of the way biologists and chemists operate. Before Crick and Watson's solution, crystallography and its resultant X-rays of DNA had yielded significant information about the nature of genetic material. Crick and Watson's problem was largely theoretical—to build a model of the DNA molecule based on structural hypotheses in turn inspired by the existing empirical evidence available in X-ray pictures. Their task was essentially to discover the shape of an existing molecular structure in terms of the arrangement of various atoms within it. Because the molecular structure in question was considered to be the basic genetic material of animal matter, the implications for the discovery are far ranging both for theory and for practical matters in medicine, organic chemistry, and a great many other areas.

Once the double helical structure of DNA was discovered, everyone working on the problem or in the field understood that the proposed solution was correct, and that any further effort would be directed toward working out the implications. As the problem initially was one of discovering a fixed structure to a biological entity, the solution sought is not of the probabilistic variety. That is, in this type of research that involves the physical and chemical basis of living matter, the structure is set and either one discovers exactly what it is or one does not. Psychological research is virtually never of this sort but, rather, is probabilistic by design. An exception in psychology is the work done in the Skinnerian tradition, and we say more about this in chapter 5.

Returning to Anderson's work, we have seen that the consistency in his results is displayed by the parallel shape of the response curves for different people characterizing others with a number of adjectives. In short, the results are not structurally relevant, they are response relevant, and therefore probabilistic in nature. Conceivably, although Anderson's results are consistent, we can imagine an individual or individuals responding to the same stimulus situation with quite different results. For example, suppose we place an unusual poet or playwright, someone like Jean Genet, in the same problem situation as that used by Anderson. It is possible that a Genet might value a bold, unsophisticated person considerably more than one who is level-headed and good-natured. If this were his response, it would break the parallel theorem. It matters not whether we can find a person that would make such a response now or not. We can imagine such a response, and having found it, it would not shock or even surprise us. This is not to say that Anderson's parallel theorem does not account for a good percentage of people's responses and the consistency implied, in placing a value on personality characteristics. It does mean that probabilistic conclusions that are useful are not the same as statements of knowledge made in other sciences to deal with their basic data. Social psychology has virtually nothing but probabilistic statements to explain social phenomena. The second implication in this analysis is that someone like Genet may at anytime respond to a social psychological situation in a different manner than he or she usually does, or differently from the majority of individuals responding to a similar situation, without this surprising us in the least. It doesn't surprise us because we understand that an individual can almost always supplant a predicted response simply by being aware of the prediction. The responses predicted by Anderson represent complicated sociocognitive processes that may change when circumstances are radically different for the individual, as when he or she is expressing themselves poetically rather than conversationally, even though they believe what they are saying in both instances.

Social psychological experimentation and theory do not develop in the same way that experimentation and theory develop in the natural sciences as illustrated, for example, by Crick and Watson's discovery of the structure of the DNA molecule. The possibility for choice that is always present in human beings precludes achieving in social psychology the success enjoyed by the natural sciences. This point is dealt with in several of the chapters that follow. What is possible in social psychology, as illustrated by the Anderson experiments and his resultant explanation, is that thoroughly probabilistic models and predictions from them can be made that are useful for practical reasons and advance our knowledge along a limited front. The problem is enjoined with the decade-old concern of Gergen (1973) that social psychology may be fundamentally historical in nature, classifying unrepeated and unrepeatable social episodes. Certainly, the limited probability assessments one makes with regard to a social phenomenon tends to be time-bound because the error accounting for the variability in the predictions tends to change with changing independent conditions influencing the social situation and the individual regarding any particular phenomenon, the most obvious example being the usually accurate, but short-lived prediction of the winner of an election. The next election, even with the same candidates participating, will involve different factors that makes reanalysis essential. In Anderson's reasonably consistent predictions over a 20-year span, the expectation that people will eventually use the same words differently and therefore render Anderson's predictions less accurate is highly likely. These natural limits on our predictions in social psychology inevitably mean that the same problems periodically cycle back into the awareness of researchers, usually in a slightly different guise. McGuire's review of this series of cycles in attitude research since World War II is a case in point.

Cycles in Research and Theory

Social psychologists have become more aware of the epistemological history of their field during the past decade than they were in the immediate period after World War II. In reviewing our field's history, the waxing and waning of interest in various research areas and in various theoretical styles of explanation reveal the nature of thinking in the field and, perhaps, some of the limitations inherent in it. The history of ideas in social psychology depicts a series of events that in themselves produce the explanation for their own existence. We can see how these cycles operate by examining certain aspects of the concept of attitude.

McGuire (1985) listed three peaks or cycles of interest in attitude research in the 20th century: The 1920s and 1930s when interest was focused on the measurement of attitudes; the waning of interest from 1935 to 1955; the cycling back of interest from the 1950s to the mid-1960s when research was conducted largely on attitude change and persuasion; disinterest during the two decades following 1965; and renewed interest in the 1980s, and presumably in the 1990s, in attitude as a cognitive system involving individual and group context.

According to McGuire there are both internal and external reasons for periodic disinterest in studying attitudes. Internal factors that tend to decrease interest in the concept are conceptual overelaboration, premature quantification, and distracting practical applications; all indicating that limits have been reached regarding the predictive and explanatory usefulness of the attitude concepts then in vogue.

Societal conditions outside of the discipline also change and weaken research interest. The changing self-perceptions of the American public after World War I and after World War II were reflected in the interest patterns of the social psychologists as well, and this produced different research interests. These are reasonable explanations offered by McGuire to account for the cycles of interest in attitude. I propose extending McGuire's analysis to the epistemological characteristics inherent in these cyclical interests that operate at perhaps a more basic level than the internal and external events listed by McGuire. The concept of attitude, like that of its predecessors, *aufgabe* and *einstellung,* is, of course a mediational idea meant to provide an explanatory step between the recognition of an external event, a social stimulus, and verbal or other behavior directed toward that stimulus by the subject.

Once we observe people classifying others into groups based on discernible characteristics, we witness both the birth of the attitude concept and a manifestation of stimulus generalization that is found in many guises among many species. Stimulus generalization is necessary for animals, including human beings, to survive by allowing a certain efficiency in responding only to those characteristics of a situation that are germane to the organism at the time of the encounter. If animals did not possess this ability they could hardly negotiate their day, so consumed would they be in investigating the individual characteristics of a stimulus in order to properly respond. When in need of a police-man, we do not question a person in an appropriate blue uniform about his training, orientation, and so forth; we assume he will act in a certain way because he is wearing a certain blue uniform. Sometimes we make mistakes, as when we assume a doorman is a policeman, but this rarely changes our tendency to generalize stimuli in a number of situations that occur daily in our lives. All behavior change is based on the assumption that organisms are capable of stimulus generalization. When the principle is applied to a human being's perception of others as belonging to a discernible group, we have a crucial part of what has come to be labeled an attitude. The addition of an evaluative component completes the concept. There seems to be no question that people do develop sets of characteristic responses to some discernible groups, for example, ethnic, political, sexual, occupational, and so on, over the course of a lifetime. The centrality of the idea of attitude as a social form of stimulus generalization that has proved periodically useful to social psychologists is established. The ability to generalize stimuli might be said to be part of the behavioral repertoire of the organism with attitude being the social manifestation. Consequently, although the concept of attitude may go in or out of favor as an explanatory device for social psychologists, the idea of stimulus generalization with an evaluative component has been fundamental in our view of human social behavior.

There are two levels at which a concept such as attitude is used. The first is as an explanatory concept regarding an aspect of human activity that is used to predict behavior or to relate some behavior to other behavior. The concept of attitude was first introduced into social psychology to account for a generalized response to group membership. If an individual was perceived as belonging to a discernible ethnic, political, religious, or other socially designated group, he or she was believed to possess certain characteristics and abilities without further analysis. Thus members of a particular group were considered to be crafty, or criminal, musical, or orderly, simply because of membership in a particular group. The assumption was that a readiness or preparedness to make decisions, to hold certain beliefs, and to behave in a particular way towards a member of a social group was learned and stored by the individual. If this readiness, called *attitude,* could be tapped by questionnaire, interview, or other method, behavior and beliefs could be predicted. To the extent that the concept works, it was used. When its usefulness diminished, it tended to disappear from the lexicon of the social psychologist only to appear again in a different form at a later date when other explanatory concepts had been exhausted.

The second level of interest to us is the epistemological level. Does the use of a mediational explanation such as attitude cycle over time in a pattern that in itself tells us something about the social and intellectual nature of human beings? This is a complicated issue and is addressed in the next chapter on historical considerations.

Applied Social Psychology

If it is accepted that there are differences between the natural sciences and social psychology in the manner in which theory is formed, then we might expect that there are differences in the way in which theory is applied to practical matters. Once the structure of the DNA molecule was discovered, work could proceed on the creation of living tissue within the laboratory. Whether one should indeed engage in such work is an ethical issue that does not affect the ability to succeed. In social psychology, a principal discovery enters into the practical situation associated with it in a somewhat different manner.

In a series of excellent studies by Aronson and Bridgeman (1979) on the "jigsaw" approach to learning in the classroom, the typical problem with applied social psychology arises. Increased racial harmony results when children are instructed via the jigsaw method, which requires that each child teach the others what it knows of his or her portion of the solution to a group problem. This technique ensures equal status contact among members of the class and produces, as a by-product, greater racial harmony compared with the usual competitive classroom atmosphere where children vie for the correct answer and whose performances are frequently compared via grades and the dispensing of the teacher's attention.

Most applied social psychological research involves social intervention and, therefore, offers the possibility for social change. These possibilities compete with other scenarios that are accompanied by different values. For example, the jigsaw technique emphasizes cooperation at the expense of individual effort and triumph in solving problems. If one values individual accomplishment, and, therefore, competition in problem solving, as many Americans do, then the jigsaw technique will be rejected even though it increases racial harmony. Indeed, some may interpret the technique as a deliberate attempt to subvert a cherished value to accomplish an end that is not as highly valued. Consequently, the emotional effect of applying the "jigsaw" procedure may be of double negative value. In other cultures where group harmony is highly valued (e.g., in Japan), the jigsaw technique might be very successful.

What Aronson and his co-workers have shown is a distinct possibility for social change if group harmony is valued above other possible values that might ordinarily compete with it in the American sensibility. If we compare Aronson's discovery with those in the natural sciences, we find that social psychological applications always require a consideration of the group value associated with the intervention as compared with its competitors relevant to the same situation. Values enter into social psychological applications as a matter of course and become part of the theoretical process itself. In the natural sciences, ethical decisions are concerned with what problem to study and whether or not to apply newly found information. The results generated in the natural sciences have no competitors with other possibilities for application, at least in the long run, as compared with those in social psychology. One *may* decide not to attempt to create life on ethical grounds, but one *can* or cannot based on the best information available in biology at the time. This is not to say that there are not controversies in the application of principals found in physics, chemistry, or biology, as whether or not one should heat a house by burning fossil fuels or by using solar heat. However, the value assessments made by natural scientists are almost always concerned with application of information to human beings, not with the empirical and theoretical solidity of the information itself. In social psychology, basic information itself can be affected by the reacting subject. For example, a child who has been trained at home to work on his or her own might inadvertently subvert the success of a "jigsaw" group. In addition, social psychology does not enjoy the kind of basic, noncontroversial knowledge that one frequently finds in the natural sciences. In social psychology there is always an alternative plan of action available at the time of application. (Do we use the best technique to insure competitive skills or cooperative skills?) Aronson et al. have demonstrated an empirical possibility consistent with the value of increasing racial harmony. It may or may not be the best technique for increasing a student's ability to understand the material in the classroom on their own. That ability is relevant to another value. This, of course, is not intended as a criticism of these studies, but rather as an illustration of the general problem of applied social psychological research. It is never value free at its very core. The value–laden quality of applied social psychology leads us to consider the idea of social context that focuses precisely on this issue.

Social Context

The idea of social context providing the missing ingredients in our theorizing has been with us for many years. Recently, the idea has been resurrected by some social psychologists (e.g., Rosnow & Georgoudi, 1986) as an alternative metaphor to be placed in the theoretical armamentarium of social psychology. The idea of context is also related to the position taken by phenomenologists and to the idea of intention discussed in chapter 4.

Social psychological reality is a product not only of measurable objective conditions surrounding the lives of several individuals, but of the relationships and agreements made among people living together. These relationships and agreements are embodied within the laws, customs, folkways, and language that are shared among people in the group. This context constitutes a reality, a condition of existence, which is as important to understand as the objective conditions in which the group finds itself (e.g., the mountain they live on, the things that are available to eat, etc.). This context is not amenable to causal or contingency analysis for the same reasons that some human decisions are not; it involves intentional responses and is a product of the unique history of the group. In short, the history of a group proceeds in a manner that is always changing, although certain of its behavior patterns may recur. The conceptual uses to which the idea of social context can be put are dealt with in chapters 2 and 6.

CHAPTER 2

Some Historical Considerations

Toward the end of the previous chapter, I suggested that social psychology must be, in part, a historical discipline—historical in the sense that the idea of the social requires time through which a group establishes the conditions under which it chooses to live. Those choices are limited by the objective conditions that constitute the physical world, and the world that it is possible to constitute given the biological nature of human beings. That is, we can create only human worlds, not the worlds of other creatures. The subject matter of social psychology develops and changes over time because change in group arrangements is inherently part of what we mean by social. The history of a social group over a sufficiently long period of time has always resulted in changes in social patterns as a result of technological invention, war, disease, and other natural occurrences. If one accepts the proposition that groups of necessity change by the very nature of group phenomena, then the question arises as to whether each group action is unique or if it follows discernible patterns. Explanation concerning social phenomena takes one or more, but not all, of the following forms:

1. A social event is exclusively part of the biological and behavioral characteristics of the human organism and is, therefore, predictable and potentially explainable by experimental analysis that excludes the historical.
2. A social event is part of a process that, although constantly changing, returns to similar forms again and again. That is, social history occurs in cycles that allow for order and universality in explaining how human beings live together.

3. A social event is part of a patterned, orderly progression of social change that allows for prediction, but without cyclical change being part of the explanatory context.
4. A social event is unexpected and unrepeatable and can only be recorded and added to other unrelated, unrepeatable social moments such as wars, political events, etc.
5. Social events follow no discernible pattern at any level of analysis.

Gergen (1973) has dealt with the fourth form, and American social psychology since the Second World War encompasses Forms 1 and 3. Form 5 removes us from the field of inquiry and for that reason alone is unacceptable. It is the possibility for cyclical explanation presented in Form 2 that provides us with a newer, fifth alternative by reintroducing the old idea that social process, although constantly changing, returns to similar patterns repeatedly. Forms 1 and 3, along with the idea of social history occurring in cycles (Form 2), allow for order and universality in explaining the nature of human beings living together. These forms assume that social activity is both orderly and that the patterns of order are knowable. The application of the techniques and concepts of experimental science to social data is the core assumption of Forms 1 and 3. The concept of cycles in the history of social affairs yields another possibility for discerning order in social existence.

The contention that social activity is not fundamentally acquired differently from any other human activity, and is, therefore, explainable by similar methods and concepts, has antecedents that are traceable at least back to the British empiricists of the 18th century. These ideas are, in turn, derivative from the Cartesian dichotomy. On that account, it will perhaps be profitable to review Descartes' (no date—modern edition) contributions.

Descartes sharpened and took as the focal point of his philosophy the Platonic notion that ideas are the most important aspect of human existence, by concluding that one was certain of one's existence if one was aware of thinking. This contention is a psychological observation rather than a logical one. Having established that one is more certain about one's own thought than about any other phenomenon, Descartes quickly followed this fundamentally subjective hypothesis with one that would serve to confuse in a number of ways. What he believed followed from the *cogitatio* was that one's own thoughts are most clear and distinct when they address themselves to mathematics and logic. He concluded that inquiry into any subject matter should proceed in a manner as consistent with the precision and clarity of mathematics as was possible. Certain epistemological points followed. Examination of the structure of thought, of sensation, and of the characteristics of objects in the world could proceed successfully by applying the same mathematical method and the same criterion of clarity. Because mind was the source of this method, it remained separate from all other possible subjects of examination. Material objects, including one's body, were seen to operate by mechanical principles and therefore, were amenable to mathematical and physical analysis. Because he believed geometry to yield the most clear and precise principles, Descartes concluded that it should be used to address every problem. He held that human wisdom is epistemologically unitary regardless of the subject matter to which it is applied.

Descartes maintained that there was a distinction between mind and body (object) and that both could be comprehended by a single epistemology. This places mind in the position of being both knower and that which is known. Descartes' separation of mind from body, both to be understood by a single epistemology, provides us with a psychological basis of knowing and burdens us with the confusion of knower being both subject and object. At the very least, Descartes established the centrality of one form of understanding with the *cogitatio,* and the separation of mind and body as subject matter. In short, his analysis provides the fundamental assumption of psychology that was to be used by many theorists from that point forward. Namely, that the individual's consideration of the nature of existence was central to the process of knowing, if not to the process of logic. For Descartes, logic and knowing are epistemologically fused in the individual when mind operates consistent with the principals of mathematics and logic, especially the analytic geometry. This position freed thought from existing scholastic modes of analysis. It produced an intellectual euphoria that usually accompanies the new and exciting, but also confusion as to how to separate an analysis of mind from an analysis of objects. The Cartesian solution was to associate the analysis of objects with mechanics and the analysis of mind with mathematics and logic, where the first was subordinate to the second.

Descartes is as impressed with the sound logical foundations of mathematics as he is disappointed in the practice to which they were put. "I was astonished that foundations [of mathematics] so strong and solid, should have had no loftier [than the mechanical arts] superstructure reared on them" (p. 43). In addition, regarding the philosophy available to him, he stated, "On the other hand, I compared the disquisitions of the ancient moralists to very towering and magnificent palaces with no better foundation than sand and mud" (p. 43). This sets the motivation for his inquiry concerning method. He sought a grand method to be used in understanding the human condition that would have the solidity of mathematics and logic. He eventually concluded that mathematics, and its handmaiden mechanics, could be applied to understanding the workings of the body, of animals, of objects in general and, indeed, of anything that cannot think. Because only humans can think, logic and mathematics are both the core of thought and the manner by which thought is understood.

In his rejection of previous philosophical positions, Descartes concluded that no idea, however absurd and incredible, had escaped the articulation of Western philosophers. Further, he noted that ideas are in and out of fashion and return in slightly altered form again and again. He concluded that the structure of our opinions is fashioned considerably more on custom and example than it is on certain knowledge. In addition, he stated that logic and mathematics are useful in speaking of things that we already know about, rather than in investigations of the unknown.

Finally, Descartes concluded that one of the methods he must use to seek the truth was to examine objects that are simple and easy to know and proceed, step by step, to a knowledge of the more complex, ". . . assigning in thought a certain order even to those objects which owing to their own nature do not stand in relation of antecedence and sequence" (p. 51).

By setting Descartes' assumptions in order, we can locate an epistemology that characterized the approach to inquiry of the 18th century, and with only some alteration, the epistemological attitude of much of our own century:

1. Mathematics and logic are both the conceptual tools of our understanding and the essence of it.
2. From mathematics are derived the principles of mechanics that can be put to use in explaining the movement of objects.
3. Human thought cannot be explained by the principles of mechanics.
4. Most of our (probably incorrect) explanations of human and other phenomena are based upon social customs that differ from culture to culture and from time to time and are likely to be cyclical in nature.
5. Mathematics and logic are successful in delineating what we already know rather than in aiding us to discover what we do not know.
6. To discover the truth about the unknown, one must begin with the simple and work to the complex by ordering all phenomena as to antecedence, sequence, and consequence,

even though some phenomena may not readily lend themselves to that ordering.

The influence of Descartes on his contemporaries and future generations of epistemologists was, of course, enormous. Perhaps his greatest influence on succeeding epistemologists was his emphasis on the possibility of rationally, analytically coming to correct conclusions about the nature of human existence by the use of principles (largely mathematical and logical) that conceptually preceded the human characteristics being explained. In short, rationality preceded existence because one could reach the truth about existence by being logical and mathematical in one's approach to it. What Descartes never accepted was that the *cogitatio* was a psychological beginning, not a logical one. Once mind and body are separated as the two fundamental subject matters of inquiry, the asymmetry of Cartesian epistemology is apparent—mind as that which knows and that which is to be known on the one hand, and body as that which is to be known by a knowing mind on the other. Extended matter (body) does not participate in the process of mind, explanation as to its workings (matter) needs to be constructed by thought (mind), and the appropriate construction for Descartes was that the principles of mechanics explain the movements of material objects.

Descartes separates pure intellection from imagination. Imagination is not part of the essence of mind as is intellection. Imagination is mind contemplating body rather than mind contemplating mind as in pure intellection. An imagining mind turns toward body and contemplates some object within it that the mind conceives or apprehends through the senses in the process of imagining. One imagines colors, sounds, tastes, and pain with less distinctiveness than when one perceives them by the senses through which they have reached the imagination. Descartes concludes that body presents qualities to mind and that perceived objects are different from thought (intellection) because they depend upon body for their origin. These differences in the origins of intellection and imagination lead Descartes to further conclude that his true essence is mind and that body is separate from it.

It follows that different epistemologies are therefore appropriate for the study of mind (mathematics, logic) and for the study of body (mechanical principles that are formed by mind). The distinction is psychologically valid, but not logically necessary. That is, we do act as if our minds (thoughts) operate by a different set of rules than does our body. For example, when we say, "I think I will go to the movies tonight," we generally believe we have stated an intention over which we have voluntary control. When we make the statement, "I have a headache," we are making a statement of fact over which we believe we have no control. We further believe that the two processes involved are functionally different ones for us. We believe we can change our decision about going to the movies at any time, but we cannot change our perception (imagining) of the objective quality of having a headache in the second statement. The question remains as to whether Descartes' distinction is epistemologically valid in any sense other than the psychological one described earlier.

Descartes left us with his belief in a clear distinction between the operation of mind or thought and the operation of body and, therefore, objects in the world. Mind was the essence of existence for Descartes and his followers attempted to work out its principles. A century later, the emphasis was to change.

HUME

Although it can be argued that David Hume was not the most important or insightful of the 18th-century British empiricists, it is clear that his thinking represented the culmination of the tradition. Writing a century later, Hume presented a kind of reversal of Descartes' epistemological position. Hume placed body or object in a central place in his epistemology where mind becomes, in part, a product of the object rather than a process independent of it.

An impression is information from the senses that may be initiated by some external object or may occur by the influence of an external object, or by some unknown process that initiates a sensation as when one suddenly has a salty taste in one's mouth without previously having eaten a salted substance. Hume's conception of an impression begins with sensation and not with an object, yet he would accept, I believe, the contention that most impressions are generated by the apprehension of an object in the environment of the perceiver. The manner in which a sensation operates he leaves to others. A simple idea is identical to, but fainter and less lively than, its corresponding impression. An idea is the faint image of an impression that appears in thinking and reasoning. Thus, if I look directly at an apple I have a forceful, lively impression of its redness and sweet aroma. Later, in remembering the apple, the idea I have of it is less vivid in both color and smell. All simple ideas are derived from impressions. Complex ideas arise out of the association of simple ideas. The three basic laws of association are resemblance, contiguity, and cause and effect. These are discussed in greater detail in chapter 3.

By 1740 there were at least two epistemological positions from which explanation of human activity could be derived. Descartes proposed that intellection was both the psychological foundation of existence and the manner by which it and the world were understood. Hume proposed that sensation was the origin of most, if not all, human action and, therefore, studying the nature of sensation provided the most certain understanding of human behavior.

Hume (1961) reversed the order of importance of impressions arising from an interaction of an object (body) with mind and idea (reflection) held by Descartes. The reversal is not precise and symmetrical because both men used somewhat different terms to describe the same processes. However, there is a sufficient difference in conceptual emphasis to warrant the distinction. Both agreed that the apprehension of an object is most vividly conveyed by a sensation (impression for Hume and imagination for Descartes). Descartes, however, did not link this observation with the strength of ideas, as the most central and important of them were produced by a different process, intellection, which is produced only by mind. Hume, on the other hand, connected impressions with both simple and complex ideas and concluded that simple ideas were both produced by and were fainter and less vivid than impressions. Hume stated,

> All abstract ideas are really nothing but particular ones, considered in a certain light; but being annexed to general terms, they are able to represent a vast variety, and to comprehend objects, which, as they are alike in some particulars, are in others vastly wide of each other. (p. 32)

Hume held that it was impossible to determine whether impressions that arise from the senses are caused by the object sensed or are produced by the creative power of the mind. In either case, the senses ultimately provide impressions that, in turn, provide simple ideas. The issue of the relationship between objects, sense, and mind is further discussed later when we consider the work of Immanuel Kant. At least two epistemological possibilities had been established with the completion of the work of Descartes and Hume. Is mind imposed, at least in part from the outside by the characteristics of objects that impinge on the senses, or is mind a condition of human existence that orders sense data more than it is ordered by it? Both Descartes and Hume appreciated the interactive hypothesis that objects (body) interact with mind (intellection) in a manner that disallows a direct answer to the question. However, the interactive hypothesis would have had to be reached by choosing a different direction. The difference in direction determined differences in epistemology that were to become more pronounced by the late 19th century. Immanuel Kant drew the lines between these two possibilities more finely.

KANT

By the time Immanuel Kant's (1961) work began, the anti-ontological seed that was contained in Descartes' work had taken hold so that direct sense experience was accepted as inextricably linked to the process of understanding. The concern with the apprehension of sense data that is found in the work of Hume and Kant, however, far exceeds the emphasis placed on it by Descartes.

Kant was challenged by Hume's beginning that sense experience was, somehow, translated into ideas (i.e., knowledge). Yet the reception of sensory data by a human being was, for Kant, missing some key ingredient that would separate mere perceiving from the ability to absorb and reuse repeatedly the data of perception that all human beings possess. In short, Kant set himself the task of accounting for the origins of any ideas that were not simple labels for a collection of Humean impressions from sense experience. His arguments and conclusions, along with his analysis of causality, are discussed in chapter 3. In summary, it may be said that Kant believed that although none of our knowledge can transcend experience, it is nevertheless in part a priori and not inferred inductively from experience. Mathematics and logic are known a priori. An empirical proposition is one that we know directly through sense perception.

How is it possible for a response to be elicited that does not have a basis in experience? Somehow, the response must be a function of a structure of some kind. That is, the structural characteristics of an object or process may produce a response that is determined by that structure, although the timing of its appearance will depend on experience (shaped behavior) and environmental conditions.

For example, we do not find strange the fact that elephants cannot fly, and the best explanation for this is that the structure of their bodies simply does not allow it. We are not surprised that our arms can bend in only one direction once we have examined the structure of the socket around the elbow. The point is that the growth of certain biological structures over evolutionary time quite often determines or limits function. Why is it not also possible that through the same evolutionary time, the human brain and central nervous system came to develop to the point where certain functions in the form of "categories of mind" or ways of perceiving objects, have developed much the same as the gross anatomy of elephants has developed and is related to their behavior?

Returning to Kant, with the completion of his work the character of the epistemology of modern psychology was set. A dialectic imperative could be formed from the positions of Descartes, Hume, and Kant.

It matters not at all that the three of them may or may not have agreed with the terms of this dialectic; succeeding generations have set it. The thesis and antithesis can be described by separate, but related concepts. What is implied by the mind–body (Descartes) impression–manifold (Kant), or sense–thought (Hume) dichotomies solidifies both the epistemological and the theoretical possibilities of modern psychology. The epistemology of psychology passed into a new phase by the late 19th and early 20th century with the rejection of metaphysical dichotomies such as those previously listed, but there was still difficulty in dealing with different conceptual strategies as they became translated into method and theory. In Freud, his highly deterministic, biologically based theory contrasts with his psychotherapy in which it is believed that a patient can alter the pattern of his or her life with a cognitive adjustment. This distinction was one of the building blocks of the phenomenological psychology of Merleau-Ponty (1963). There was, in addition, a distinct effort made by the early behaviorists, particularly Watson (1913) and Lashley (1923), to eliminate the last vestiges of metaphysical and epistemological mind–body dichotomies by embracing the principle by which psychological theory was to be built by considering only the behavior of the organism as the essence of its psychological life. The organism's biological characteristics and proclivities were bracketed to be studied in another context.

The mind–body dichotomy, or any of its derivatives, was a bother to psychologists of the late 19th and early 20th centuries. Because of the success of experimental science and its attendant epistemology in areas such as physics, chemistry, and biology, psychologists looked for a form of monism that would allow them to duplicate the success enjoyed by the natural sciences. The elimination of mind was an early, if cautious choice (see Lashley, 1923) of the behaviorists. Their epistemology was adapted from the British empiricists, particularly David Hume. Sense data became the primary material of their science. Objects in space and an organism's behavior with regard to them were the units of study. This tactic allowed one to redefine mind as verbal utterings, themselves convertible to behavior that shared equal epistemological status with any other behavior of which the organism was capable. This eliminated the possibility of the organism making a decision (choosing a behavior) independent of a *specific* connection between the behavior and a reinforcing element. However, no theorist, since and including Kant, would say that an organism can make a decision not connected to the environment in some way. Later, Skinner was to attempt to handle the problem of self-reinforcement, as in the acquisition and use of abstract words and phrases, by invoking the "autoclitic" as a special aspect of verbal behavior. But more about this later.

This strategy, to eliminate the mind portion of the mind–body dichotomy, was necessary to determine whether or not theory could be developed to explain human existence with the same success as had been accomplished in the natural sciences. Although the strategy was honorable and necessary, it failed. It failed because it eliminated half of Descartes dichotomy in the manner suggested by Hume's work, but without considering Kant's contribution to the solution of the problem. Those psychologists more influenced by Kant than Hume, among whom we may count the gestalters, Merleau-Ponty, and some of the later existential therapists, tried to solve the problem by attending to immediate experience as the sine qua non of human existence. Eventually, with the rise of interest in human cognitive facility in the 1980s, the old mind–body problem evolved into a behavioral–cognitive dichotomy, but with the issue regarding the nature of thought still not settled. Behavior remains behavior so long as it is not cognition. However, is cognition behavior in that it is the product of a reinforcement sequence, or is it a self-generating activity of the human machine? We explore that issue in chapter 5.

The influence on modern psychological epistemology of the mind–body dichotomy and its modern offspring are largely accepted by psychologists as a periodic issue. However, explanation of social phenomena may need separate treatment if social psychology is, as was suggested at the beginning of this chapter, in part a historical discipline. The epistemological origins of this contention can be usefully attributed to the work of Giambattista Vico, particularly as it was a reaction to certain aspects of the Cartesian position.

VICO

By 1710, Giambattista Vico voiced his objections to Descartes' metaphysics. By 1725, Vico produced his major work, *The New Science* (1961), which extended the key concepts of *verum* and *certum* first expressed in, *On the Most Ancient Wisdom of the Italians* (1988). Vico's contribution, therefore, follows Descartes and precedes that of Hume and Kant. Vico's ideas differ significantly from the metaphysics and epistemology of Descartes and, therefore, also from that of Hume and Kant. This departure provided an early conceptual basis for a different epistemology regarding social existence that is at the center of some of today's issues regarding how to proceed in the field of social psychology.

Vico made a distinction between the true and the certain. Truth (verum) seeks to understand universal and eternal principles. It is the pursuit of the a priori. Reason, logic, and mathematics are major elements of verum. Mathematics is understandable and can lead to the discovery of the truth because it was made by human beings. That is, the nature and content of mathematics is not observed in, and gleaned from, the external world. It is constructed by human thought, and provides us with clues as to how thought operates. However, the premises of mathematics are fictions that need not conform to any principle or to the nature of any natural phenomena. Therefore, mathematics lacks the same level of reality that is present in the physical world or the social world. The physical world was not made by human beings, hence it can only be understood in a limited way. Physics is not capable of ever producing verum (truth), but can produce certum (certainty). Certum refers to contingent facts and, therefore, to probability functions. Because humans made a social world, that is, laws, customs, and language, they are capable of reaching verum by studying it. In addition, the principles of social existence, unlike mathematics, are not fictions, but are part of the living human world. Therefore, these principles are different from those of mathematics although both are capable of yielding verum. The principles of social existence also share the characteristics of the physical world in that one must begin the pursuit of understanding the social world by the pursuit of certum.

The distinction that Vico made between verum and certum is in large part an attempt to correct the weakness in the Cartesian criteria of clarity and distinctiveness by which one judged the truth of a proposition. Clarity and distinctiveness referred, of course, to the psychological condition of the thinker with regard to the truth of the idea being assessed. Vico's proposition of differences in certum and verum required separate epistemologies for study of the external world compared with study of the internal or ideational world. In short, certum was the goal of the natural sciences, and verum the goal of metaphysics, mathematics, and, unique to Vico, etymology. His etymology was also essentially social as it involved an examination through the evolution of language of the development of jurisprudence and other social customs unique to a group of people living together.

If we examine Vico's distinction between certum and verum within our contemporary context, the ideas are both useful to us and in need of some alteration. Verum can be reached by understanding the processes that we invent, such as mathematics, and our social customs and institutions. Certum is reached by examining that which we do not make, that is, nature. Natural science yields, certum and mathematics and social science yield verum. We can, perhaps, accept the Vichian differences between the certainty of mathematics via proofs, as mathematical systems are tautological, and the natural sciences that require observations of objects and processes occurring outside of our own tautological inventions. However, placing what we can know about social process alongside of mathematics rather than the natural sciences is unacceptable to most modern theorists. Social science is an empirical enterprise and, if anything, is less successful in reaching verum than mathematics or the natural sciences in their pursuit of certum. Did Vico really believe that understanding language, jurisprudence, and social customs could gain the same level of success of mathematics? I believe that he did. This is not a proposition, however, with which I agree. However, there is something in these distinctions that Vico proposed that suggests differences that are valid in the different epistemologies that accompany mathematics, natural sciences, and social inquiry.

The issue rests with the differences in approach of social inquiry compared with either natural science or mathematics. Rather than two epistemologies characterized by verum and certum, there are three: mathematics, the understanding of the true because it is totally deductive and tautological; natural science, the understanding of objects through contingency analysis; and social science that is in part like natural science because some social facts can be analyzed probabilistically, and in part like the study of mathematics because human beings make decisions unaffected by any specific chain of contingencies regarding the terms under which they will interact with others. People create language, mathematics, and social convention. Social scientists can describe those creations, as Vico was wont to do.

Vico's new approach was historical, philological, and focused particularly on the human customs and sensibilities that developed at the dawn of particular civilizations and that, therefore, preceded the methods of philosophers and scientists. Vico provided an explanation of the nature of the social soil from which mathematics, logic, and science grew. He was concerned with the social foundations of nations (language groups) that preceded the development of their rational laws and customs. Vico believed that a universal set of social principles was attainable because nations, unknown to each other, nevertheless held a common ground of social truth because, as humans, they confronted the same problems of existence. Understanding the myths of a nation through an analysis of the development of its language is necessary to lay bare this groundwork. It is by language that ideas concerning customs, laws, and the sense of being human are carried, and it is language in a neverending cycle that provides the definition of life itself. Rational, logical, mathematical, or scientific ways of using language are preceded by simpler, more fundamental uses of language. Simple metaphors are found very early in the development of a language and usually refer to parts and functions of the body: foot for end, head for top or beginning, the tongue of a shoe, a neck of land, the hands of a clock, and so forth. In this sense there are rules that take the form of universals, in that their materialization, although specific to a time and place, nevertheless indicate the historical commonality of using the body to describe the world. Vico is the author of the historical view of humanity.

It is within this historical context, with philology (we invent words and their meanings) serving as method, that Vico's major contribution to understanding the nature of society is contained. When his concept of the social in its historical context is compared with our more familiar epistemological forms, his contribution is most obvious, and the direction for modern social psychology implied in it becomes apparent. Vico pointed out that the Greeks and Romans, in an attempt to explain the nature of their societies, produced a mass of contradictions and general confusion. They failed because, instead of examining the concrete processes of their own history and deriving universals from the cycles of that process, they attempted a transcendent analysis yielding principles of social organization based on extended metaphors too general to capture the actual nature of their societies.

Human beings are present to themselves as ideas only as part of their idea of society. No other concept is possible as an individual exists always within the social context, and all terms of reference in self-description are social. A woman may be a mother, a provider, a professional, a wife, and so on. Consequently, what is most basic in the social is a subject existing in a sociohistorical context. This subjectivity is eliminated by the natural attitude and restored by the historical. The attempts by Bacon, Hobbes, and others to reconstruct, apodictically, the social process by which people made covenants with one another based on abstract principles of social organization (Hobbes, 1651/1904) in order to construct a society misses entirely the true history of groups. The concrete process of social history is what gives rise to attempts to explain it apodictically rather than social organization being founded by rational covenant.

The duality between positivity (the concrete instance) and ideality (an abstracted principle of operation) needs to be closed. It is closed by allowing the concrete context of social history to reveal the abstract principles that become apparent by the recurrence of certain events over time. One, however, begins with the context in its concrete reality. For Vico, some examples may serve to illustrate this crucial point. Special forms or customs are the ligatures of community and have developed from its collective early experience. They can be abstracted and codified as ideas as part of the cycling back to a specific form during the history of a group.

Because the first principles by which humans lived preceded those of the rational philosophers, these principles were the natural laws of the people developed from the way they formed their original lives together. The human custom of burying one's dead indicates that one knows one's kind; being monogamous allows one to know one's children and thus provide them with inheritance and oneself with the "immortality" of progeny. These are part of the original act of consciousness that formed society then and as we know it today, and that preceded abstractions about it. These social principles are the beginning of language, the development of the mind, and the onset of social existence.

Myths in the cultural life of a society are instances of self-expressions by which a culture knows and defines itself. These images are dynamic and immediately enter into a dialectical interplay with other images that continually transform the sense in which a community knows itself in the most basic form. These images separate a people from the chaos of nature from which they emerged. Vico conceived of humanity itself as a process of ideas and institutions "coming to be" at certain times and in certain places. The progression through which humanity changes has certain characteristics that proceed from the ingenuity of youth through the maturity expressed in restrained rationality and eventually back to the chaos of early times. In short, mind does not precede language, but arises with it, and both are the outcome of the social necessity to grasp experiences through familiar images.

The ideas of God and his powers, the burial of the dead connected with the idea of immortality of the soul, and the institution of marriage to insure a sense of origin and perpetuity, are three such recurrent forms that, of course, exist even today. They are identifiable as eternal verities concerning the character of all groups because of their cyclical nature and because the concrete realities that underlay them occur in every group. It matters not whether God actually exists or whether the soul is immortal or whether origin and perpetuity are real in the natural sense. What matters is that these forms are part of the living subjective reality of social existence.

It follows for Vico that the science of social process does not exist outside of the process itself. Social psychology is a moment in the process of society unlike, for example, the science of physics, which is not such a moment—except in a trivial way—of the process of objects in space. The methods and concepts of social psychology are only abstract for convenience, not, as in physics, by necessity. The science of physics, however, does exist within the social world and exists as part of it as a useful metaphor for explaining the nature of objects that are themselves part of the social world, but not of it as subjects.

Vico's idea of social history cannot be transformed into naturalistic terms, as the process of history does not occur as an order of cause and effect. Human beings cannot fully comprehend physical nature precisely because humans know it as an order of cause and effect, or as a series of contingent events. Cause as a metaphor can be applied only to events that can be objectively perceived, because events in a cause and effect sequence require that each be identified as a discrete entity whose principal characteristic is its temporal and spatial relationship to another event or events.

Cause is admitted into Vico's analysis of history as it applies to a specific series of events occurring in a particular place at a particular time in the history of the group, those events being determined by specific conditions, of which he seeks the universal principles of temporal order and appearance and nothing else.

What is required at this point is to indicate how the substance and spirit of Vico's position is relevant to modern social psychology, while preserving his distinction between the sense of history compared with that sequence in natural science and with abstract principles of philosophy in general.

My intention in this section is to compare and contrast the Cartesian tradition with Vico's position so as to suggest ways of increasing the power and expand the horizons of contemporary social psychology.

Vico and Descartes Compared

Descartes' ideas enjoyed the same success as the science of Galileo and Newton. His emphasis on mathematics as method and mechanics as the proper science of objects epistemologically justifies the efforts of 17th- and 18th-century scientists, including those interested in human activity. The difficulties imposed by Descartes' mind–body dichotomy were resolved in the 18th century by eliminating, in one form or the other, one of his two methodologies. At first, an emphasis was placed on, and later, an explicit commitment made to, mechanical concepts in explaining human activity. Descartes would most likely have been appalled at the result, but the success of causative mechanical explanation in nonhuman sciences was a tempting approach for psychological explanation. Consequently, 19th- and 20th-century science, and eventually psychology, developed as causative, linear, contingent, objective approaches to understanding. The experiment with its controls and dependent and independent variables became science's principal method.

Nineteenth-century introspection was replaced by a mechanical system used to explain behavior (Rosnow, 1981). In the early 20th century, what worked was fruitful in the development of psychological explanation and prediction was part of the mechanical legacy of Descartes. The other half of the legacy, characterized by introspection, failed, because although it looked in the right place, it attempted to combine incompatible elements—the causative unilinearity of science with the ideation of the traditional philosopher.

That aspect of the Cartesian spirit in American psychology has unquestionably enjoyed a certain success; it is therefore crucial that we acknowledge this, and that we do not reject its contribution, in particular to social psychology, even though it has definite limitations. All experimental research in social psychology is potentially useful in characterizing social arrangements within severely time–bound situations. The results of experiments provide checks and balances to our views at a given moment. The results of experiments in social psychology, however, cannot *by themselves* be used to develop relatively long-term principles of social life, if Vico's hypothesis is true. If social phenomena are truly understood historically, then the history itself must somehow generate the terms of explanation of its substance. In short, social phenomena are historical in a manner in which physical phenomena are not.

If Vico was correct in his objections to Cartesian epistemology, and was also correct in his articulation of the principles of verum and certum in his new science as a set of attitudes and methods whereby one could come to understand the social nature of human beings, then certain precepts follow. Social phenomena are understood:

1. From human experience or context in toto;
2. As fundamentally noncausal, that is, they cannot be understood by application of causal reasoning (Buss, 1978; Lana, 1969, 1976);
3. By examining the rules (laws, customs) of a social group that are transmitted by language and the way it is used, as the development of language reflects the development of the socius;
4. By considering social context as it occurs and as it is lived as the fundamental "unit" of study. Context is not further reducible to component parts, unless for purposes of analysis that have nothing or little to do with the understanding of social development. Also, this context yields the meaning, indeed *is* the meaning, of social reality.

As with so much of psychologists' search for routes for their endeavors, we are still modifying our concept of the proper unit of study for the field. For the gestalters it was the perceptual whole; for the later behaviorists it was the observable bit of behavior linked to contingencies of reinforcement that are also observable. Vico's etymological historicism renders the search for a proper unit of study no longer necessary. Units of study (an attribution, belief, attitude, etc.) still have their place within the causative, contingent concepts associated with social behavior, but they are not useful if we wish to understand the meaning of social interaction for the participants.

How is one to proceed in examining social content in order to build a solid body of information and knowledge? Description of rule–following behavior (Buss, 1978; Lana, 1969; Lana & Georgoudi, 1983; Winch, 1958) is a necessary process. Vico's model is informative. As we have seen, he analyzed explanatory metaphors in the early development of language, as well as analyzing Greek and Roman myths and what they revealed about the civilizations in which they developed and about universal social reality. One must, in short, interpret the meaning of social context. One observer's interpretation may or may not ring true to another person, but it can always be appreciated as an instance of subjective reality, which thus may act as a *possible* living context for the person for whom it is not now reality. By gathering the commonalities present in repeated interpretative assessments of social reality, one may come to learn the fundamentals of its perception. This approach remains forever distinct from the approach of natural science appropriated by psychologists from physics and biology. However, the distinction between the two methods—natural science on the one hand, and history and hermeneutics on the other—provides a genuine dialectic that, although never reaching a thoroughgoing synthesis, allows for conceptual progress. It is Vico's elements of certum and verum, certainty and truth, and their dialectical relationship, that produce the synthesis that yields a more complete understanding of social phenomena, but never fuse epistemologically or, therefore, methodologically.

Vico's Cycles

Vico believed each nation's culture evolved independent of all others. Cultures and nations followed sequences of development that are given by discoverable universal principles. These principles become manifest only within the sweep of history. The beginning of this sequence can be understood by analysis of the language of the ancient myths of a nation.

The poems of Homer, the first coherent written record we have of the history of a Western people, represent civil history as well as catalogues of the customs of the ancient Greeks. The law of the 12 tables of the ancient Romans serves as a similar database. Analyzing those, as Vico did, gives us a picture of the origins of two societies. The common nature of human institutions can be understood by analyzing the "mental language common to all nations" (Vico, 1961, p. 25). This common mental language, or common perception of reality, "grasps the substance of things feasible in human social life" (p. 25) and expresses this in a number of different ways in different languages. To trace the development of a word is to trace the history of an idea.

The construction of laws and the development of language accelerated the speed at which a society changed. The development of language also interacted greatly with the development of social institutions and customs. Vico concluded that the changing structure of language reflected the changing structure of thought and of society. For example, human laws unattached to the idea of a divinity are unknown in the Western World. With the connection between divinity and public order, it is natural to develop the concept of a hero who combines the qualities of divine origin, strength, and bravery. Vico pointed out that every Western nation had its Hercules.

There are three fundamental cycles of human development in Vico's view. The first he called *poetic,* the second *heroic,* and the third *human.* At the beginning of social existence, reasoning is weak among the people and form is given to society by theological pronouncements based on the group religion. Consequently, the governing body is theocratic, deriving its power from the divine and holding it by piety. Divine ceremonies prevail that give rise to government by those who understand the divine mysteries. In ancient times, these priests were said to enter into the mind of God. Revelation is the manner through which God's will is understood by certain people who then interpret it for the multitude. At the familial level, the father is judge. Communication through writing is by mystical hieroglyphic signs.

When a poetic age is established, it provides the basis of the next cycle of human social history. The priests of the poetic era eventually arm and think themselves to be of divine origin. They regard the plebeians, who have not received the Word, to be bestial in nature. The governing body is aristocratic, with a choleric, punctilious approach to governing. Force controlled by religion is given voice by heroic blazonings, as in military speech. As an example, "The blood boils in my heart" communicates anger. Universals are described by reference to myth, as Achilles is a sign for valor and Ulysses a sign for cleverness. Understanding divine mysteries as a means of constructing laws in the poetic age gives way to law by precise formula. Jurisprudence develops in a manner that carefully uses the proper words and expressions to make legal points so that the formula of the law is satisfied. The letter of the law is supreme.

The final stage of human social development occurs when the plebeians revolt to insure rights for themselves encompassed by the aristocratic auspices. Marriage allows property to be passed on to one's kin and assures other rights as within the aristocracy. It is then that human intellect and reason culminating in the development of rational laws takes hold. Language develops into a vulgate. Laws are developed by reason and made applicable to everyone, not simply the aristocracy. Heroic speech ("The blood boils in my heart") gives way to the vulgar ("I'm angry"). The truth of facts allows the bending of the rule of law to the equity of the cause. Science is born because reason and logic prevail.

Eventually this final stage decays because its very success in obtaining the goods and rights that people desire changes the structure of society. In addition, the reasoned laws of this final stage become abstract and unconnected to social reality. This decay leaves society open to encroachment by a group at an early stage of development and the cycle begins again.

A return of societal forms and sensibilities is cyclical in the manner of a moving spiral returning to its origin, but always at a different level than the previous cycle. The spiral analogue also captures the dialectical aspect of the idea of Vico's cycles—each phase creating its antithesis and ultimately the synthesis being achieved at a different level. The repetition of social explanation parallels repetition of the developmental cycles of the social group in its concrete experiences. That is, Vico's position is epistemological as well as a description of concrete, historical, social reality. The cycles are part of the way people perceive the nature of social reality and, therefore, abstractly define themselves as a result.

Observation of this human social context can be characterized by an alienating distance of the observer (Gadamer, 1975) from that which is observed. This is necessary for objective analysis, but it destroys the primary relation of belonging to the group observed. The observer has therefore altered or eliminated his or her relationship to the group and to the historical per se. The result is a paradox of alienation, a tension between proximity and distance that is essential to historical consciousness and that Vico embodies perhaps more than any other observer of societal process.

Besides there being historical cycles of social activity, there are cycles in the explanation of social reality. Vico expects change in the nature of social analysis that will parallel, in dialectical form, actual social changes. This follows from his point that language both reveals and creates the terms for change and progress in future description.

As we have seen, Vico began his major work as a reaction to the dominant Cartesianism of his day. He concluded that the Cartesian system was limited in a crucial way. This limitation is found in a conceptual area apparently ignored by Descartes: the social. Whereas Descartes claims that error results from cycles of human explanation arising from social custom, Vico based much of his system upon such cycles of explanation (Lana, 1986). That is, Vico accepted change as categorical. For Vico, the history of social reality preceded and gave birth to the methods and concepts that are central to Descartes' system. Vico sought to supply the missing ingredients of linguistic and philological content. Vico's arguments can be summarized as follows:

1. Mathematics and logic, although constructed by human thought, need not conform to any principle or to any natural phenomenon. They lack the same level of reality as that of empirical science.
2. An empirical science such as physics is concerned with the operation of objects and is known in a different way than mathematics, but incompletely (they are known only probabilistically).
3. Social facts are both empirically observable and are constructed by humans, and hence are known in a third way different from the other two.

It is this third way of knowing that constituted Vico's *New Science* (*Scienza Nuova*). This new science was historical, philological, and focused particularly upon the human customs and sensibilities that developed at the dawn of particular civilizations and that therefore preceded the methods of philosophers and scientists.

Vico tacitly assumed that human beings are limited in the way they can react to one another. As a result, they develop similarly even though one group may not actually influence another group even if it has contact with it. It is these human limitations that give rise to the concept of social cycles. For example, it is impossible to succeed in building a commercial city without the citizens losing a good deal of their enthusiasm for soldiering as a result. When this occurs, another cycle is already in the process of developing. Without the limitations of human reaction suggested by the idea of cycles, humans would be gods, a proposition Vico is not willing to accept.

By the 18th century, the opposition between the logician and the rhetorician reached a peak that was followed by the triumph of the rational and the submergence of the social, prelogical aspects of human existence. Currently, the social has risen again even within social psychology, which had lost it for about 40 years.

As we have seen, Vico believed that the cycles of social change are paralleled by cycles of explanation about social change. These explanatory cycles occur because of the difficulty of a theorist maintaining both the social distance necessary for disinterested analysis while also participating in, and being sensitive to, the very society he or she is attempting to describe. This is an issue that is of singular importance to modern social psychology as we see in succeeding chapters.

It has been pointed out (Morawski, 1986) that modern, positive social psychology has ignored history and language. Language and common rhetoric within the larger historical context may yield universal principles of human society. The repetition of certain elements of social action in different guises may allow us to glean the rhetorically and linguistically carried principles that are not discoverable by means of positive causal analysis, unaffected as it is by social history. The history of social reaction to, for example, death in a given culture, particularly noting changes over time, may reveal certain enduring principles of social organization. Marriage and education are other candidates for such an analysis.

Modern social psychology has, until recently, abandoned the subject and the history of the subject's discourse with others. A subject is constituting of the life that he or she leads. The person creates it and is influenced in this creation by other people. If this constituting attribute of human beings was understandable by reference to a causative, contingent set of observations of the individual's behavior alone, any analysis or theory of social activity would be impossible. Because theory and analysis are constituting, social acts in themselves, the only question that remains is what elements of human activity *are* usefully described by causative, possibly mechanistic, analysis.

Difference Between the Historical and the Behavioral

In the analysis of behavior, behavior is treated as if it is nonhistorical in the sense that knowledge of the past history of the organism, although this history contains the reinforcement sequences that have produced the organism's current behavior, is not essential in changing behavior. That is, an organism's behavior can always potentially be changed by applying new reinforcement schedules.

The truly historical requires that the particular history of an individual or group of individuals have both a current behavioral component and be consciously integrated by the individual or group so that past events and their interpretation are verbally reviewable and have stated values associated with them.

A value assessment of past events that influence behavior patterns in the present may not be recoverable, as when someone may not know the historical origins of, for example, a celebration, nor understand why he or she believes the celebration to be important, but knows that it is important. Knowledge of an individual's group history may allow an observer to predict and understand, in a historical sense, the person's behavior.

In nonhistorical positions such as behavior analysis, for example (chapter 5), knowledge of the individual or group's history is not essential in order to change behavior, even though that past history may contain the reinforcement sequences that have produced an individual's current behavior.

CHAPTER 3

Causation

One of the natural derivatives of the Cartesian dichotomy is the separation of causation from intention in the epistemology of modern psychology. For a human event to be caused, and to discover that cause, implies that it is no different from the events in other sciences and that, therefore, the epistemologies of psychology and the natural sciences are the same. If a human event is not caused, one need consider the person as the origin of the event and the individual's intention regarding that event is of central importance. Consequently, the methods of psychology would be different from the methods of other sciences.

In this chapter I discuss the nature of causation as it implicitly or explicitly enters psychological theorizing. Intention is discussed in chapter 4.

CAUSE AND EFFECT

Determining the nature of causation has occupied a number of people for a long time, but there is still no general agreement as to its definition (Tooley, 1987). The concept enters psychological thinking, either implicitly or explicitly, in a way that it does not enter thinking in biology, physics, or chemistry. This is because psychological prediction and explanation require that one take a position on the nature of causation both as a process by which one builds explanation, and as a characteristic mode of responding of human beings who are the builders of explanations of the world around them.

Sometimes, as we see here, questions as to the nature of causation are admittedly begged and a kind of causative agnosticism is acknowledged. In other instances, the nature of causation that is assumed in an explanatory system is made clear. In either case, psychologists, social or otherwise, must deal, at some time or other, with the issue.

It has been argued repeatedly that:

1. Causation is a characteristic of human reasoning, a description of a particular kind of human experience involving relations among objects (an epistemological characteristic).
2. Causation is a relationship of objects to one another that is so perceived by human beings (an ontological characteristic).

Both assumptions, of course, could be true. We recognize the empirical manifestations of the first proposition in that human beings, in our experience, make frequent observations of aspects of the world that involve inferences from presumed causes to presumed effects. Analysis of this first assumption often takes the form of examining whether or not people legitimately (i.e., logically) can make such inferences. The second assumption is more difficult to assess as our own observational and logical characteristics interfere with determining whether or not nature acts in a causative mode all of the time, some of the time, or none of the time. If either the epistemological or the ontological positions are true, a second important issue is to determine whether or not the causative idea is relevant for all events or only for some events.

Some definitions are in order (Bunge, 1959). *Causation* refers to the causal connection in general and to any particular causal connection or nexus. The statement, "A thrown baseball produced the broken window" is an example of a statement of causation. The *causal principle* refers to the law of causation that holds that the same cause always produces the same effect. The statement, "Baseballs thrown swiftly against windows invariably break them" is a causal law implying the causal principle. Causal determination is the assertion of the universal validity of the causal principal; in short, the position that everything has a cause. I use *causation* and *cause and effect* interchangeably.

Causation as Constant Conjunction or Necessary Production

This point of view is exemplified by the proposition, "If C (cause) then (and only then) E (effect) always." This formulation does not allow us to make a distinction between propositions of the types (a) "Continually administered aperiodic punishment causes maladjustive behavior," and (b) "Hooded rats have better visual acuity than albino rats."

The first statement is directly causal; the second asserts a correlation between two qualities that may or may not involve direct causation. The statements are not intended to convey the same kind of relationship in the usual way they are used, yet both fit the definition of causality as conjunction.

An informal definition of the idea of causation involving necessary production is given by Bunge (1959): "If C happens then (and only then) E is always produced by it (p. 47)." The effect does not merely succeed the cause, or accompany it, it is brought forth by it. Causation as constant conjunction is a tacit statement concerning an epistemological characteristic of human beings, whereas the idea of causation involving necessary production is an ontological statement that requires a lawful arrangement of the relationship of some objects to other objects regardless of the human view of them.

Causation as an issue of epistemology was, of course, set by the work of David Hume and Immanuel Kant in the 18th century. To grasp the essence of the problems confronted by both men is crucial to our current understanding of inference making in social psychology.

David Hume

The concern of the British empiricists from the late 17th to the late 19th century was to determine the content and process of mind through an analysis of perception. The analytic spirit of a now full-blown natural science allowed the empiricists to consider mind as composed of elements or units, which they labeled *ideas.* An idea was the object of thinking, and mind was analyzable into ideas. In becoming interested in the content of mind, the question that next naturally arose is how ideas become connected to one another to form the ebb and flow of thought. The association of ideas through various rules of combination had already been discussed by Aristotle and was taken up by Thomas Hobbes, John Locke, and David Hume.

For John Locke (1690) ideas were generated from two sources, sensation and reflection. Because an idea can come from sensory experience, objects in the outside world are directly transmitted to the content of mind. This involves the various organs of perception such as the eyes, ears, and nose, thus an intrinsic linkage was established between the generation of an idea and the functions of various parts of the body. Locke also held that it was possible to have an idea about something without actually having perceived it in the first place. Certain ideas, such as those of mathematics, were not perceptual in origin. He concluded that the mind knows its own processes by reflection.

Ideas are either simple or complex. Simple ideas are unanalyzable, but complex ideas can be analyzed into simple ideas. The principles by which simple ideas are combined to form complex ideas are the rules of association. David Hume (1961) adopted Locke's explanation of impressions and ideas and from that base constructed the observations and arguments that were to bring him to his monumental discovery concerning the nature of causation.

Every simple idea has a corresponding simple impression, although complex ideas do not necessarily have corresponding complex impressions. Simple ideas are combined and connected through the process of association, which is brought about by resemblance, contiguity, and cause and effect (causation).

Resemblance. The presence of one idea introduces or determines the recall of another because of similar elements existing among ideas.

Contiguity. When two ideas appear together in space and time the presence of one calls up the idea of the other.

Cause and Effect. The combination of cause and effect occurs when the presence of one idea (or event) seems to necessarily compel the appearance of another idea (or event). This is the most forceful of the three conditions of association. It is also a concept that Hume found difficult to comprehend.

Following is a summary of Hume's analysis:

I.   All simple ideas are derived from simple impressions that correspond to them and that they represent.
(a) These impressions and ideas are in constant conjunction, therefore, the impression may, but does not necessarily, cause the idea it precedes in time.

II. Two objects that are perceived as cause and effect have the following characteristics:
(a) They are contiguous in space and time.
(b) The cause occurs before the effect.
(c) There must be a *necessary connection* between cause and effect in order to differentiate causation from mere (accidental) contiguity.

Hume rejects the conclusion that the effect is produced from a cause on the grounds that the idea of causation involving production (the cause compelling the effect) is reducible to IIa and IIb (contiguity in space and time and the cause preceding the effect). That is:
(d) It is equally valid to assume that an object may exist

without it having been caused as to assume that it necessarily would have had to be caused. To assume that an object had to be caused to exist is to assume the validity of the idea of production as an essential ingredient in causation and not a proof of it. Hume rejected the idea of production, as we have seen, in IId on the grounds that it reduces to the principals of IIa and b.

(e)   Therefore, the idea of necessity in causation is not a function of reasoning logically, rather it issues from the experience of the individual that gives rise to the idea of necessity in causation. The idea of causation is, therefore, an epistemological attribute of human beings.

(f)   Causation as a human process extends beyond sense impressions to unobserved events as when we come to expect an object or event to be present or occur when we make a prediction based on an observed object or event. For example, I predict that the sun will rise tomorrow (unobserved instance) based upon the fact that I notice that it is dark now (observed instance).

III. The nature of the experience that yields our idea of causation is determined by:

(a)   An impression or an idea of an object and an impression or an idea of another object.

(b)   The idea of the connection of the two by causation, that is, one object causing the appearance of the other object.

  1. It is not known whether the original impression of an object arises from the object, from the individual, or from God. (This is the basis of Kant's later noumena–phenomena distinction.)

  2. No object implies the existence of another—it is the ideas we form of them that does because of our experience.

IV.   Necessary Connection. As we have seen, reasoning cannot account for necessary connection between cause and effect according to Hume. Even though the constant conjunction of the cause with the effect is required for our *perception* of causation, we cannot legitimately conclude that there is a concurrence between the objects we have observed in a causal relationship and those which are beyond our observation because they have not as yet occurred (as when we make a prediction). We do make predictions about unobserved times based upon a belief in the causal connectedness of objects we have observed.

(a)   Even though he established that causation is an epistemological aspect of human inference characterized by contiguity, succession, and constant conjunction, Hume concluded that it is only of value in allowing us to make correct inferences if it somehow corresponds to a natural relation among impressions and, therefore, ideas. In short, causation is a useful idea if it has ontological as well as epistemological status, Hume has put it this way:

> The idea of necessity arises from some impression. There is no impression conveyed by our senses which can give rise to that idea. It must, therefore, be derived from some internal impression of reflection (remembered thought; parentheses mine). There is no internal impression which has any relation to the present business, but that propensity, which custom (habit) produces, to pass from an object to the idea of its usual attendant. This, therefore, is the essence of necessity. Upon the whole, necessity is something that exists in the mind, not in objects; nor is it possible for us ever to form the most distant idea of it, considered as a quality in bodies. Either we have no idea of necessity, or necessity is nothing but that determination of the thought to pass from causes to effects, and from effects to causes, according to their experienced union. (p. 152)

Summary of Hume's Position on Causation

Because the power by which one idea produces another idea cannot be discovered by examination of either one or both of the ideas involved, it follows that cause and effect are relations of which we receive information from experience and not from abstract reasoning. According to Hume, causation depends on the epistemological characteristics of the inferrer rather than on the characteristic of the objects seen as cause and effect (the ontological position). When two objects are present to the senses and a relation of one to another is perceived by the observer (e.g., one object appears behind another object), this perception has nothing to do with reason. It is directly given where the mind (thinking) need not go beyond perception to comprehend the relative position of objects to one another. In contrast, the experience of cause and effect requires understanding to go beyond immediately given perception and utilize the idea of necessary connection between the two objects. From this, we are at least assured that the perception of one object was followed by the perception of another object.

If we observe the constant conjunction of two objects or their constant remoteness from one another, there is nothing in the objects themselves that allows us to conclude that they are always in this relationship. We do conclude that there is a yet undiscernible cause that unites or separates them. Of the three relations producing the association of ideas (resemblance, contiguity, and cause and effect) only cause and effect involve processes beyond our senses. Causation is an idea involving two objects, thus it followed for Hume that it must have an accompanying impression. Clearly, such an impression cannot inhere in any quality of the two objects involved in cause and effect because they are simple objects that can be found in noncausal relations. The idea of causation, therefore, must be derived from some relation among objects.

Hume concluded that objects need to be contiguous in space and time in order to be perceived in a causal relationship to one another. As has been noted, the principle of contiguity is also a characteristic of association, without necessarily implying causation. Simple ideas can be associated by means of contiguity in space and time without the idea of cause and effect emerging. However, the basis of a complex idea of causation is also that of contiguity in space and time. In addition, Hume considered that all objects can be either a cause or an effect. His position can be stated:

1. All objects can be cause or effect.
2. Any two given objects in contiguity with one another in space and time often produce simple ideas of association, but not necessarily ideas that involve cause and effect.
3. Two objects perceived in a cause and effect relation to one another are always contiguous in space and time. The cause always precedes the effect.

Hume rejected the classical idea that the cause produced or compelled the effect because he could discover only contiguity and order in the cause and effect relationship. On those grounds he rejected the logical legitimacy of the classical concept of production of the effect by the cause. It therefore followed for Hume that every object that has a beginning does not necessarily have a cause. He argued that we can imagine a nonexistent event for the first time without the principle of necessity being conjoined in the process. It therefore can be assumed with equal facility that an event occurs with a cause or that it occurs without a cause. Hume recognized, nonetheless, that people hold to the idea of necessary connection between cause and effect. As the idea of necessary connection is neither derived from logical reasoning nor directly observable, the question arises of how individuals experience an idea of causation. Apparently some type of experience forces the notion of the necessity of an effect following a cause. Hume never resolved this issue to his own satisfaction.

In retrospect we are not surprised at Hume's impasse regarding the concept of necessity in the concept of causation. Given the firmly entrenched empiricism of his day with the accompanying emphasis on sense data as the origin of epistemological and ontological consider-ations, his conclusion was foregone. With some exceptions, he be-lieved the process of thought to have characteristics that were the same as those of the objects of sense. If an idea could not be accompanied by an appropriate object–impression, the idea itself was suspect.

Kant

Immanuel Kant (1961) was intrigued with Hume's analysis and began work on the problem of necessity as Hume had left it. In dealing with the relation between cause and effect and necessary connection, Hume reached a significant conclusion. Because any idea arises from an impression, or is a combination of simple ideas, the idea of necessity must either arise from some impression or be a combination of simple ideas that themselves have arisen from impressions. Hume indicated that there is no impression that can yield a legitimate idea of necessity in the external world. He also concluded that there was no combina-tion of simple ideas that could form the complex idea of necessity. The tendency for people to make causal inferences was, therefore, a result of a psychological propensity in the individual that allowed him or her to pass from the impression of an object to the idea of the object, which is the condition that accounts for the idea of necessity.

Kant was challenged by Hume's analysis. Hume's work once again raised that most important question regarding human knowledge: To what extent does an understanding of the nature of objects differ from an understanding of the nature of human thought? In all statements where there is a relation between subject and predicate (e.g., The cat is black), either the concept P belongs to the subject S, or P lies outside of the sphere of influence of S. In the first instance, Kant called the relationship "analytical" and in the second "synthetic." Analytic state-ments involve a predicate that is contained in the idea of the subject, whereas synthetic statements add something to the idea of the subject by the pronouncement of the predicate. "All bodies are extended," is an example of analytic judgment, and "All bodies are heavy" is an example of synthetic judgment. As analytical statements serve only to clarify existing knowledge and do not add to it in any way, synthetic statements are generally of greater importance.

Both Hume and Kant took direct experience as the starting point of their epistemologies. However, the fundamental units of that experience are quite different for each of them. For Hume they are impressions and ideas; for Kant, the fundamental units are the act of synthesis and the given manifold. Kant agreed with Hume that the principle of causality is neither self-evident nor capable of logical demonstration. Either Hume's skeptical conclusions must be accepted, or we must be able to indicate some criterion that is not dependent on experience, but on which experience itself is dependent.

In each of its momentary phases experience can be analyzed into an endless variable material called (a) the manifold, which comprises the content of sensation; and into (b) a fixed set of interdependent relational elements that are the forms of sensibility (called "forms of intuition"), the categories of the understanding, and the ideas of reason. As these relational elements are synthetic (Hume's influence is apparent here), they can be established only as essential conditions of our sense experience. As these relational elements are absolutely necessary for the structuring of our experience, they are a priori. A priori is both a necessary and a relative concept; necessary in that human experience has this particular structure, and relative in that human experience of the world is not an experience of the world as it is in itself, but as it is necessarily for us. The a priori relational elements are therefore as strictly factual as the experiences that they structure.

Kant proposed three levels of reality:

1. An ultimate reality (called "things-in-themselves" or "noumena") that transcends and generates human experience but is unknowable.
2. A realm of appearances (the phenomenal world), which is the objective, experienced world *common* to all *human* consciousness, but not reducible to the merely subjective states of individual human beings.
3. A realm of purely private imaginings.

The irreducible relational elements in the objective, experienced world, as mentioned earlier, are the forms of sensibility, the categories of the understanding, and the ideas of reason.

The forms of sensibility are space and time. These are pure forms of perception that are not generated by empirical perceptions, but in fact are presupposed by them. Because sensations differ only qualitatively (a basic Kantian assumption), the form of space must be added by the mind, producing "side-by-sidedness" and extension of objects. Space must be a necessary representation a priori, for it is impossible even to imagine the absence of space, although it is perfectly possible to imagine space as existing without objects to fill it. Because space must be "thought away" or "perceived away," it must be a priori, that is, a necessary relation of appearances to one another in the common world of appearance.

The a priori aspect of time is demonstrated in much the same manner, although time does not determine the relation of appearances to one another, but only the relation of representations in our inner state. The idea of time does not originate in, but is presupposed by the senses. When a number of things act upon the senses, it is only by means of the idea of time that they can be represented as simultaneous or as successive. The notion of time, even if acquired through experience, cannot adequately be defined as a series of actual things existing one after another. For one can only understand the meaning of "after" if he or she already knows what time means. As time is an a priori relation, we cannot know whether or not it is a relation of things-in-themselves (noumena). Inner processes are not known with any greater certainty than are outer appearances.

The second set of irreducible relational elements is the 12 categories of the understanding. These are 12 intellectual forms that may be contrasted to the pure forms of sensibility previously discussed. Certain pure forms, or categories, originate in the understanding. These categories combine with the perceptual forms of sensibility and the variable manifold of sense–contents to produce the consciousness of an ordered experience. For our purposes, the most crucial of these categories is that of causation.

In order to demonstrate how the category of causation is necessarily presupposed in the consciousness of an ordered experience, Kant distinguishes between the consciousness of the merely subjective order of our apprehension and the consciousness of the objective flow of events. He gave two examples. If we apprehend a house by successively apprehending the different parts of it, there is no necessity to begin at the roof and then go to the basement. We could start at the basement and work our way up to the roof just as easily. We would not regard either of these sets of successive perceptions as representing anything characteristic of the house. On the other hand, if we see a ship gliding down a river, our apprehension of its place higher up in the course of the river must come first. It is impossible in the apprehension of this phenomenon that the ship should be perceived first below and then higher up. Here, the order of the succession of our apprehensions is determined and our apprehensions regulated by that order. In the example of the house, there was no order in the succession of perceptions determining the point where we had to begin, whereas in the apprehension of the ship gliding down river, the order of successive perceptions was necessary. We are compelled to apprehend the ship going down river. We cannot reverse at will the order and apprehend the ship going upstream as we can reverse at will the starting point of our perception of the house. In order to distinguish objective succession from subjective succession, we must regard the former as compelling to our perception; that is, in order to be apprehended as objective succession, it must be understood as necessitated by causal connections. The category of causality is a logical presupposition of the objective succession of objects or events in time. All possible experience, that is, all objective knowledge of phenomena with regard to their relation in the succession of time, depends on the category of causality.

Although Kant limited the principle of causal connection of phenomena to their succession, he found, as a practical matter, that it applies also to their coexistence, because cause and effect may exist at the same time. If we look at a ball that rests on a soft cushion and makes a depression in it, we see a cause simultaneously with its effect. We nevertheless distinguish the two. If we place the ball on a cushion, the cushion's smooth surface is followed by a depression, whereas if there is a depression in the cushion, a ball by no means follows from it. The *irreversible* sequence relation remains even if there is no interval between the two events. It is this irreversibility that is the decisive consideration.

It is also necessary to distinguish between the causal principle and specific causal judgments. We have been discussing the general principle that every event must have some cause in that which immediately precedes it. What, in each instance, this cause is can only be discovered empirically, and one can never be absolutely certain. Kant would agree with Hume that even though we are confident that it will, we do not really have a basis for saying that the sun will absolutely rise tomorrow. If wax has melted, we know a priori that something must have preceded that event (e.g., the heat of the sun), after which the melting has followed according to a law, although without specific experience we could not know a priori either the cause from the effect, or the effect from the cause. Kant would insist that Hume was wrong in inferring the contingency of the causal principle from the contingency of specific causal judgments. Although we cannot be sure what causes the wax to melt, it does not follow that something does not necessarily cause it to do so. The category of causality enables us to predict a priori that for every event there must be some preexisting cause, but only through empirical research can we pinpoint the specific cause.

The third set of irreducible relational elements is the ideas of reason. The categories of the understanding and of causality are limited to experience, for the categories are merely forms for relating phenomena and are in themselves empty. For instance, the attempt to prove the existence of God through the concept of causality would be impossible because it would be extending causality beyond experience. The principle of causality dictates that in our sensibility, that is, in space and time, every condition that we can reach in examining given phenomena is again conditioned (not in the modern sense as a learning process, but in the sense of "having conditions attached to"). These phenomena are not objects by themselves in which something absolutely unconditioned might possibly exist. The categories place the data of perception into relation with one another in such a way that every phenomenon must necessarily be thought of as being conditioned by other phenomena. Every phenomenon has its conditions, which leads to an infinite regress. Reason, however, is unsatisfied with this infinite regress. It seeks to reach the unconditioned itself, the self-caused that contains in itself the conditions for all phenomena. The ideas of reason and mental representations of the unconditioned arise because human reason extends beyond merely attempting to discover phenomena and understanding them as *our* experience. It is the object of reason to ascend from the conditioned synthesis to which the understanding is always restricted, to an unconditioned synthesis beyond the understanding. Pure reason never refers directly to objects, but to the concepts of objects framed by the understanding.

Kant was concerned with the conditions of perceptual truth. He never provided an answer to the question of the relationship between perceptual truth and the world of objects in themselves. For Kant, the actual nature of the objective world was unknowable. However, there is an objective order to sensible phenomena. This order may have no connection with the order of objects as it exists in itself. This perceptual objective order is known when it follows from the invocation of a rule allowing that order and none other in the perception of the individual.

By way of summary, it may be profitable to point out some of the salient features of Kant's idea of causation. For an event to be distinguished from a subjective series of sense apprehensions, it must be conceived to have been caused by another event. Thus perceptual objectivity may be produced by cause and effect. The temporal order of the events, causally linked, is the essence of the objective event. Kant sought the necessary and sufficient conditions that would allow objective perceptual truth to be apprehended by the perceiver. Unlike Hume, who stressed the psychological qualities of the concept, Kant attempted an epistemological argument for the validity of the objective idea of cause and effect. Kant's idea of objective apprehension begins with the notion that experience is translatable into sense perception only through epistemological considerations. Cause and effect as a principle is presupposed by all judgments about the world of fact.

The work of Hume and Kant on the nature of causation set the modern dimensions of the concept. What remains is to integrate this legacy with the scientific method as it was perfected in the nineteenth and twentieth centuries. In turn, this allows us to finally relate causation to both the nature of psychological theory and to the nature of the propensity to think causally in human beings.

Causation in Science

A causal law (an instance of the causal principle) (Bunge, 1959; Russell, 1962) is any general proposition that allows us to infer the existence of one object or event from the existence of another or several other objects or events. The objects and events are sense–data. Over successive applications of the causal law, the specific objects and events will be different, but the relationship among them will remain the same. A certain relationship among classes of objects is the essence of the causal law. In a causal statement, the temporal condition of the pertinent events or objects must be specified because the object or event from which another is inferred (cause) bears a specific time relation (either prior, antecedent, or simultaneous) to the object or event inferred (effect). The contiguity among the relevant events or objects leads the organism to expect certain results specifically because of it. The expectation is the same as that mentioned by Hume in his psychological analysis of causal inference natural to all individuals. Bertrand Russell (1960, 1962) referred to this expectation as an animal belief in causality, and notes that it can be observed in horses, dogs, and other animals. This psychological propensity usually results in identifying one event or object as cause and another as effect. This identification is more primitive than the idea contained in the concept of causal law, which involves a statement of invariance and not merely an expectation of succession.

In the usual use of the terms *cause* and *effect,* the cause is seen to be invariably prior to the effect. However, the concept of causal law allows temporal priority neither to the events or objects identified with cause, nor to those identified with effect. There is no valid inference one may make with respect to expectations of future events based upon observed relevant contingencies in the past. That is, there is no characteristic of the contingency of events in the past that allows one to make the logical jump to expectations of events in the future, although there is a psychological tendency to do so.

How then is any empirical statement of a causal law to be verified or interpreted as meaningful? To state that all future consequences of a general proposition are true is itself a proposition of which the specific instances cannot be enumerated. If I hold that the table exists only when I look at it, and another holds that the table exists when neither I nor anyone else is looking at it, the testable consequences of both hypotheses are exactly the same. If meaning is to be identified with verification, then these two hypotheses have the same meaning. It is clear that the two hypotheses should not have the same consequences and, therefore, that seeking the meaning of a proposition in its consequences leads only to other propositions and so on, through an infinite regress (Russell, 1962). The difficulty lies in an insistence on experience for inference and verification. We must have some reasons in advance of experience for believing that some given event will occur. Inference of something not experienced is not inference of something nameable, but rather the truth of an existence proposition. If causal laws are valid, in whatever cases, it is possible to know existence propositions without knowing any particular instance of their truth. The work of Hume and Kant have led us to the position that all synthetic knowledge (in Kant's sense) is based upon experience. Yet we have statements such as, "There is an event which no one perceives," which are meaningful to us. We can comprehend a sentence whose subject matter lies outside of experience because it uses words that are variables (in a mathematical sense) and have meaning within other experiences that we have had. The words I understand are understandable through my experience. However, the truth or falsehood of the statement is not apprehensible through an understanding of the words in the sentence. What is required is that we have some knowledge of universal propositions that will allow us to judge the truth or falsity of statements that are not just existence propositions involving statements of empirical probability. Universal propositions based upon perception alone apply only to the period of time taken up by the perception, and cannot indicate what is occurring when we are not in the act of perceiving. Those elements of cause and effect that constitute the necessary conditions (of connection between cause and effect) for successful inference are the universal propositions. These propositions or postulates cannot be deduced from the facts of experience, as has already been demonstrated. "Either, therefore, we know something independently of experience, or science is moonshine" (Russell, 1962, p. 505). Experience must be supplemented by causal principles involving necessary connection that are known a priori, in order to infer the existence of future, unobserved cases.

How then does the a priori category of Kant and the human tendency to infer to unobserved instances of Hume function within the modern context of predictive science, and to what extent is this human proclivity reflective of the orderly operation of the universe? The assignment of meaning to statements that imply a cause and effect relationship between two or more events or objects may be understood within the context of theory construction in science, and especially in psychology.

Induction by simple enumeration is not sufficient to establish the generalizations of science. A generalization must be considered within the context of the scientific system of which it is a part. The method by which we establish hypotheses within a scientific system is therefore of central importance in discovering meaning within the system. It must be shown how the constant conjunction of two or more events with the addition of a doctrine concerning the use of generalizations in a scientific system can be combined so as to account for the idea of necessity in the causal sequence while minimizing the use of a priori assumptions. An inductive hypothesis of simple antecedence of cause from effect is taken as well established if it has not been refuted by experience and has been confirmed by a number of positive instances, in accordance with some minimum expectation established as a policy for that induction. The principle of elimination holds that an inductive hypothesis is taken to be well established if it has not been refuted by experience and if alternative hypotheses have been refuted by experience. The linkage between the subjective validity of making an inductive inference and its objective validity, which mirrors a contingent characteristic of the universe, is the effectiveness of the belief in the validity. Effectiveness is, in turn, established by a confirmation of an expectation held by the inferrer (Braithwaite, 1960). Any law-like statement of invariance between two or more events or objects gains validity from one or both of two sources: The statement's instances are validated either by induction, or by their holding a necessary position within a series of logically and empirically linked statements that, in their most complete form, will be hypothetico-deductive. It is now possible to conclude that the nature of the elusive concept of necessary connection between a cause and an effect is attributable to the logical position the cause and effect inference holds in a coherent system (theory) of similar, related statements. Any derivable empirical consequence of a hypothetico-deductive system can and must be validated by recourse to induction by simple enumeration or one of its variants.

However, unless the rules of logical deduction are in turn made amenable to inductive verification, simple enumerative induction involving the constant conjunction of a series of events cannot alone account for the total meaning of a causal statement. Because any generalization within an established deductive system appears as a deduction from higher level hypotheses that have been established independently of the generalization, the process of generalization cannot be validated by the evidence evaluating the higher level hypotheses. These principles of connection must be established by different evidence, that is, by other principles. As we have seen, it would be difficult to show that the validation of these principles is based upon induction. Consequently, we are turned back again to some form of validation by a priori principles.

The idea of necessity in causation cannot validly be derived from constant conjunction. It is inherent in the deductive schema and its attributes that form the connective linkages among inferential statements in a theoretical system. The question arises as to whether or not a causal statement based upon the constant conjunction of events can legitimately be causal if it is not contained within a deductive system. It would be difficult to imagine the statement having any law-like properties, however, if it were not so contained. For example, we might observe that the number of professors and the number of mules in several states were inversely correlated, but the fullest meaning of this observation would be found in an analysis of the states' agricultural, educational, and sociopolitical structures. Our original statement of constant conjunction would be "explained" when placed within a system of related statements of which it was a derivative expectation. "The nature of scientific laws cannot be treated independently of their function within a deductive system" (Braithwaite, 1960, p. 339).

Causation and Inference in Psychology

Psychologists do not have the luxury that the natural sciences have of permanently separating epistemological issues from the issues associated with their primary subject matter. Indeed, epistemological issues constitute the primary subject matter of cognitive psychology as well as important data for clinical, developmental and, social psychology. The process of causation and its role in inference enters the concern of psychologists at various levels. Those levels are discussed here.

Level I: The Ontic Level. The Ontic Level is an effect expected from a cause on the basis of a necessary relationship between the class of events called cause actually preceding invariably the class of events called effect. The relationship is further established by being contained within a logically coherent set of related statements called *laws* that constitute a predictively successful theory (e.g., any one of Newton's six laws of dynamics). There are no such known laws within the subdisciplines of traditional psychology. One of the very few attempts to construct a hypothetico-deductive theory within traditional psychology similar to successful ones in physics, was made by Clark Hull (1943). Actually, Hull made two such attempts, the hypothetico-deductive theory of rote learning, and a similarly structured theory of general behavior. Hull defined theory as:

> . . . a systematic deductive derivation of the secondary principles of observable phenomena from a relatively small number of primary principles or postulates, much as the secondary principles or theorems of geometry are all ultimately derived as a logical hierarchy from a few original definitions and primary principles called axioms. (p. 2)

His magnificent effort was to fail completely, but not without instructing those who followed in what was possible and what not in the formation of explanation concerning psychological entities. Hull's goal was to develop theories of behavior as sound as those he saw in physics. His belief in the ontic character of possible psychological theories was as certain as that of successful theoretical physicists. This ontic certainty, as we can appreciate from his definition of a scientific theory, was synonymous with the successful prediction of phenomena from a logically coherent theory. In turn, I have suggested that the theory context of a causative statement is what provides the idea of necessity in the causal inference. As well conceived as Hull's system was, it failed because he could not make the consistently successful predictions about animal behavior that he had hoped he could. It would remain for B. F. Skinner, working with behavioral data as Hull had, to move from an ontic causal level to another, more conservative epistemological position.

Level II: The Epistemological Level. This level is the assumption that attributions of causation are made by all people periodically throughout their lives and that this fact is a manifestation of their epistemological nature. Whether or not this universal epistemological characteristic has an ontologically secure base or not is another issue (Level I). The nature of this epistemological characteristic of assuming that some events (C) cause other events (E) such that the effect follows the cause necessarily, is then explained by references to the nature of the inference. We have seen how Hume and Kant have provided related epistemological explanations of the process of causation as exercised by human beings perceiving certain phenomenal arrangements in their environments. These attributions of causality must conform to the expectations of Level III as follows, but not necessarily to the expectations of Level I (see Fig. 3.1).

Level III: The Agnostic Level. The Agnostic Level is a successful inference from one event E_1 to another following event E_2 based on the previous constant conjunction of the two events. The E_1-E_2 observation is not embedded within a hypothetico-deductive system nor any theoretical system that contains laws linked empirically (inductively) and logically (deductively). An example of these inferences is the family of curves representing different schedules of reinforcement and the response rate associated with each in a given species. The curves are used by the experimenter to predict behavior only, and not to develop a set of logically interlocking propositions as in Level I. Causation as an ontological or epistemological category is bracketed at this level and no assumptions are made as to its nature or even as to whether or not it is a valid concept. The issue of whether it is valid or not to make an inference to an unobserved time by depending upon the constant conjunction of two events is not considered, and only the usefulness of so doing for practical purposes of prediction and manipulation are considered important. In short, this level of inference eschews the question entirely of the nature of causation or inference making. The question of whether or not the successful predictions made by inference from the constant conjunction of events is reflective of the actual character of the events in reality is also eliminated. This is a very conservative epistemological position that depends solely on the ability of the scientist to predict an event from another so that the information is useful in some manner. It is a legitimate position if no reference is made to the nature of human beings making such inferences nor to the underlying nature of the events entering into the predictive formula.

Level I assumes the validity of Levels II and III in that the agnostic

FIG. 3.1. Assumptions regarding other levels requried by each inference level.

Level I (ontic)	LEVEL II (epistemological)	LEVEL III (agnostic)
Assumes Validty of:	Assumes Validty of:	Assumes Validty of:
Level II	Level III	
Level III		

position regarding the ontic certainty of causation at least requires that the observer accept constant conjunction of instances of the cause followed by the effect to be useful in prediction, and that the epistemological interpretation of causation be true of human inference making in order to accept the ontologically secure quality of causation.

Level II requires that the Level III assumption of constant conjunction of events considered to be causes with events considered to be effects is a practical way of making successful inferences to the future. In short, relying on the constant conjunction of cause with effect is a condition of causal inference that is a human epistemological characteristic. Level III, of course, need not assume the validity of Levels I and II.

Causal Inferences Regarding Social Activity

The social psychologist raises further questions that are independent of a consideration of the logical validity and empirical usefulness of the human tendency to make causal inferences:

1. An individual's attributing causality to a sequence of events may be correct from a scientist's vantage point, but the person making the attribution may not know why it is correct because he or she is unfamiliar with the arguments of Levels I and II. The social psychologist is interested in this attribution of causality because it is a universal social phenomenon.

2. An individual's attribution of causality is incorrect, but it is still of interest to the social psychologist because it is an example of error in the attribution of causality to various social events that may form patterns of response in a given society.

3. An attribution of causality in which it is impossible to invoke Level I and therefore to judge whether it is correct is not the issue, but the social process of attribution of causality is, as in Level III. If someone crosses the street against a traffic signal and is struck by an automobile, a causative explanation of the event is possible, but chance can play a role, as people who cross against the traffic signal are not invariably or even frequently struck by automobiles. However, many people will make a causal attribution as to whom caused the accident. Regardless of whether people make causal or chance attributions on a logically and evidentiary secure basis, the fact that they make them at all is of social significance.

The discussion of the nature of causality is, I believe, necessary to indicate the possibilities and limits of predicting and theorizing about social activity. Social psychologists do not have the luxury of ignoring epistemological and ontological issues for very long if they are to succeed in understanding, or at least predicting, social phenomena of various kinds. Obviously, all human beings engage in some form of causal thinking regardless of whether or not it is predictively or theoretically successful. That fact alone places social psychologists in a more difficult position than practitioners of most other scientific disciplines because it requires that they (social psychologists) use the very processes they are examining to make analyses and conclusions about them.

ERNST MACH AND THE EPISTEMIC–ONTIC SEPARATION

Ernst Mach (1959) provided one of the most influential solutions to the ontic–epistemic issue by addressing Kant's noumena–phenomena dichotomy.

> Thus, perceptions, presentations, volitions and emotions, in short the whole inner and outer world, are put together, in combinations of varying evanescence and permanence, out of a small number of homogeneous elements. The aim of all research is to ascertain the mode of connection of these elements. . . . For us colors, sounds, spaces, times . . . are provisionally the ultimate elements whose given connection it is our business to investigate. (pp. 22, 29–30)

The colors, sounds, and so forth, are inherent neither in the physical objects involved, nor in the characteristics of the perceiver, but are products of the interaction of the two, rendering a separation of epistemological and ontological considerations unnecessary. Mach sought the functional relations among experiences. Any reference to things-in-themselves (noumena), or to any variable outside of interactive experience, was superfluous.

For Mach, complexes of colors, sounds, and other sensations, called *bodies,* are denoted by the letters A, B, C. . . . The complex of colors, sounds, etc., which is part of the former complex (A, B, C . . .), but that can be distinguished from it by certain peculiarities, is denoted by K. L. M. . . . The complex composed of memory images, volitions, feelings, and others is represented by α, β, γ. . . . In common, but incorrect thinking, the complexes α, β, γ . . . K, L, M . . . , taken together, are conceived as the ego. The ego is thought to contrast with bodies (A, B, C . . .) existing external to the other two sets of complexes. At first glance, A, B, C . . . appears to be independent of the ego and opposed to it with a separate existence. However, many changes in α, β, γ . . . do pass by way of changes in K, L, M, . . . to A, B, C . . . , and vice versa.

The group A, B, C . . . always is determined in part by K, L, M. . . . The physical characteristics of an object depend on the conditions within an organism, and upon the relations between object and organism (e.g., distance, light available) at a given time. In short, the nature of perception makes the idea of the separation of object and organism, of object and ego, extremely difficult to maintain. "The properties of one and the same body, therefore, appear modified by our own body; they appear conditioned by it. But where now is that *same* body, which appears so *different?* All that can be said is, that with different K,L,M, . . . different A,B,C, . . . are associated" (Mach, 1959, pp. 9, 10).

Thus the fundamental datum of science for both physicists and psychologists is sensation. Mach's position is that the observational and inferential processes of all science are the same. That is, the perceptions of the scientist are subject to the same laws whether he or she be psychologist or physicist. However, in psychology, sociology, and anthropology, the subject matter is often indistinguishable from the scientist's observational and inferential processes, compared with the subject matter of the natural sciences that is easily distinguished from the processes of the scientist studying it. Contrary to Mach, this may make a difference in the kinds of inferences made by social scientists. If one follows Hume and Mach to the behaviorist tradition (chapter 5), it is allowable that dealing with human activity proceeds in essentially the same way as a physical scientist dealing with the data of moving objects. One may observe human behavior, record it, and organize the results in the same manner a physicist would when observing the movement of a planet. On the other hand, when the subject matter is the reasoning process of the scientist, the scientist's approach is itself part of the process he or she is studying.

THE EXPERIMENT

A scientific experiment, in many ways, is a remarkably simple event, yet it sustains a power and elegance apparently out of proportion to this simplicity. The idea of an experiment is to recreate a part of the world in a controlled manner. A control implies that an experimenter is able to manipulate key aspects of the experimental situation. The degree to which these manipulations are quantifiable is the degree to which the experiment is precise. Difficulties with the applicability or meaning of experiments depend on the bit of the world that the experimenter has chosen to examine under these controlled conditions. If it is trivial or if it is irrelevant to his or her purpose, the experiment to that extent is useless or less useful than it would be were he or she able to recreate a significant or meaningful bit of the world in a controlled situation. It is usually the case that the more precision the experimenter can maintain in the experimental situation, the less important problem he or she is studying. Conversely, the more important the bit of the world brought into the experimental situation, the less able one is to control precisely the elements of the experiment. This is particularly true when human beings are the subjects of the investigation.

A human subject maintains his humanity in an experiment. He perceives that he is perceived by others within the framework of the study. In short, he knows he is in a study. This makes the individual's phenomenal world (in the Kantian sense) relevant to the meaning of an experiment, but not necessarily to its method. An experiment is not applicable when a problem involves an individual's sense of his or her place in the world. If it is desirable to teach someone to do something quickly and efficiently, such as learn how to drive an automobile, experimental research on that subject will be very helpful. What the individual learns may be a bit of important information, yet it may not touch his or her sense of self. If it does, as in the situation where someone thinks he is more manly because he can drive a car, it does so because the individual has interpreted the learned act within a socio-personal context that places a value upon it. However, this fact is not contained as a variable within the manipulations used to teach him to drive. With the reader's indulgence, a brief review of the structure of a simple experiment will allow us to continue the discussion, making shared assumptions about the experimental process.

An experiment has one or more independent variables, which are those events quantitatively manipulated by the experimenter. The dependent variable is the event (or object) that is presumably influenced by the manipulation of the independent variables. It is the event in which the experimenter is principally interested. The extent to which the experimenter is able to precisely control the independent variables is the extent to which their effect on the dependent variable will most precisely be measured. However, the relevance of the independent and dependent variables to the information that the experimenter wishes to gain is problematic and not contained as a variable within the framework of the experiment. It is more influenced by the imagination and ingenuity of the experimenter. Control is accomplished by applying the rules of logic both to the total structure of the experiment (as in the need for a control group of subjects) and to the conclusion drawing that is made about the results of the experiment.

The Subject

If there is one fact of experimental life that social psychologists understand as a result of the past 20 years' research on artifacts in experimental design and the controversy that followed, it is that the subject in an experiment is active rather than passive in his or her receipt of the experimental manipulations. As discussed previously, artifact research (e.g., Rosenthal & Rosnow, 1969) was, for a time, a growth industry. As we have seen, one of the results of the controversies that arose was that some social psychologists worked harder at developing experimental techniques to eliminate the acknowledged artifacts in experimental design, and another group essentially abandoned experiment as the principal means by which one could come to predict and build theory about social existence. Current activity (e.g., Gergen, 1973) in the field indicates that supplementary forms of approach to understanding social phenomena have developed. The monolithic dominance of the experiment is no longer as evident in social psychology as it was in the days of Carl Hovland and the Yale group.

The acceptance of the active subject forces a reconceptualization of the nature of social activity and reintroduces concepts such as intention, and phenomenal (noncaused) existence back into a consideration as nonreducible human qualities. Considering the active subject in relation to others requires a further assessment of whether to tacitly assume that a radically different approach to understanding is necessary or if human science needs to be expanded beyond the foci provided by various forms of behaviorism, psychoanalysis, etc. Is there a significant difference between social science and the natural sciences or are they contiguous along the two dimensions proper to science—its empiricism and its mathematization? An alternative to the experiment that widens the epistemological scope of social psychology is yielded by phenomenal description and hermeneutic analysis (chapter 6), especially as applied to social history. The problems coalesce around the fact that there is a prescientific *lebenswelt* (Husserl, 1960, 1964, modern version; Vico, 1961, modern version) that not only influences the process of proper science, but is the very subject matter of social psychology. The *certum-verum* distinction of Vico leads us in this direction as well.

There are proponents of the position that *geisteswissenschaften* is necessarily epistemologically and methodologically different from *natur-wissenschaften* (e.g., Habermas, 1971), and there are proponents of the position that such separation between the epistemologies of natural and social sciences is not conceptually possible (e.g., Spence, 1956). All would agree, however, that any conception of science must be broadened beyond that of mechanical or merely causal explanation to include the more recent conception of natural science. Whatever the merits of these arguments may be, and they are considerable, I take a different tact and examine closely those social phenomena labeled *historical* and *intentional* and the necessary reflexivity (see following chapter) of social theorists.

CHAPTER 4

Intentions

It has been said (Cioffi, 1982) that the clarification of intentionality should be the principal function of clinical and social psychology. One position (Follesdal, 1981) is that rationality is the key to intentionality. In turn, rationality requires a consistent and solid empirical foundation in establishing one's beliefs that may be followed by appropriate behavior. B. F. Skinner (1976) has also taken the position that intentionality is the key to predicting human behavior and believes that his system of behavior analysis is an effective way to accomplish this task. Intention also arises as a possible factor in accounting for potential discrepancies in social psychological predictions such as those associated with Anderson's data (chapter 1). If these observations are correct, it follows that an analysis of the intentional process in human beings is essential to account for the difference that exists in what it is possible to know in the natural sciences and what it is possible to know in social psychology.

Intention is a process that refers only to human beings in that it indicates a proposal of what one will do in the future. Often, but not always, there is a goal one wishes to reach as in the stated intention, "Tomorrow I will begin my new exercise program." Statements of intention are communicated symbolically, usually verbally, thus we do not ordinarily speak of the intention of animals, although in some higher forms, such as chimpanzees, we sometimes believe that rudimentary intentional behaviors are possible. Ultimately, the concept is linked with verbal report or the possibility of verbal report, thereby making it an essentially human phenomenon. Accepting this contention immediately separates a study of intention from all other scientific endeavors, especially those associated with theoretical analyses in physics, biology, and chemistry. What remains is to discover whether scientific methods and concepts akin to those used by the natural sciences (Ryan, 1970) can also be used to successfully analyze human intention.

There are several related issues to consider:

1. The relation between intention and causality.
2. Whether intention is always conceptual, that is, cognitive in nature, or whether it can be analyzed exclusively by referring to behavior.
3. Whether intention can be utilized by an individual to adjust environmental imperatives.
4. Whether intentions are rational in that their behavioral concomitants are consistent with environmental realities.

INTENTION DEFINED

The position taken by the late 19th- and early 20th-century phenomenologists provides us with a conception of intention that centers it as the most important human reaction. Brentano (1973) and Husserl's (1964) contentions regarding intention continue to be debated to this day, but it is possible to consider what intention means and what it does not for the purposes of clarifying social action.

A prediction ("I am going to get a cold") is different from an intention ("I am going to go for a walk"). A distinction must be made between the two types of statement. Prediction and intention both make reference to the future so this cannot distinguish them. The statement "I am going to go for a walk," is the expression of an intention whereas the statement, "I am going to get a cold," is an estimate as to what will occur in the future. A single utterance can be an intention, an order, and information, as in, "The third base coach will give the steal sign." This is not an estimate of the future based on evidence, as in a prediction. It can be seen as an intention (of the team manager), as information from the manager to his team, and as an order of the manager to his team. An order is not the expression of an intention, but rather the description of action cast in a special form. However, commands and expressions of intention are similar in that they both suggest what it would be good to make happen with a view to an objective.

If I do not do what I said I would do in the expression of an intention, it cannot be said that I have made an error, as I have, had an estimate I made been incorrect. It also cannot be said that I lied. That is, one can say, "I will go for a walk," and having not gone, not be said to be necessarily lying. A lie is a statement contrary to one's thought. The truth of a statement of intention is not a matter of doing what one said. The truth of an expression of intention is only to believe the intention when one is uttering it. A command is a sign, whereas an intention can exist without a symbol. We speak of commands, not expression of command, but we do speak of expressions of intent.

In order to understand expressions of intention, we need to consider something internal, that is, what it is an expression of. This consideration disinclines us to call such expressions, "predictions," that is, the description of something in the future.

What an individual actually does is of primary importance in considering intention. An intention involves someone knowing what he is doing under the terms that he knows. "I intend to steal second base," "I did not know that the coach did not give the steal sign." Intentional actions are those about which we can ask the question, "Why?" The question "Why?" is not applicable to a situation where evidence for a sequence of action can be invoked. "I saw a spider crawling over the table, which made me jump and that is why I knocked the coffee cup to the floor" (Anscombe, 1957). This is an estimation after the fact of a sequence of events that might have looked like intentional action to an observer, but which is not to the actor when he explains his actions in the manner indicated.

The issue arises as to the ontological status of an intention. Mental phenomena that are object-directed are distinguished by the fact that their objects need not exist (as in considering green elephants). For Brentano, intentionality means the object-directedness of thought. Therefore intentionality is a feature of phenomena and has phenomenal existence. For the British linguistic philosophers (cf. Chisholm, 1957), intentionality is a feature of language and therefore mental phenomena can succeed in achieving objective reference. Somehow, both of these conceptions of intentionality need to be preserved in our conceptualization in order to bridge the thought-behavior gap that invariably arises within this context.

In intention, there is reference to a content; there is direction applied to an object that can be a thing or an object of thought (a green elephant) that does not exist as a thing. A mental phenomenon, characterized by intention, includes something as an object within itself. No physical phenomena have the characteristic of intention; therefore, intentionality is part of the response repertoire only of human beings. (Perhaps there is rudimentary intentionality in the higher animals.) The possible nonexistence of the object of a mental act (thought) is what distinguishes it from physical phenomena. Brentano, for one, concluded that a descriptive psychology was necessary to adequately deal with mental phenomena characterized by intention. Descriptive psychology is not the same as the empirical psychology we are accustomed to in contemporary America. Empirical psychology is concerned with the causal connections between physiological conditions and behavior and between behavior and its environmental consequences. Descriptive psychology deals with the first person perspective, that is, the workings of the mind or thought that are not reducible to thing-relationships on the argument already presented. The act of mentally presenting is different from that which is presented, and the appearance to consciousness is different from external or physical phenomena that enter the life of the individual. From this phenomenological prospective, empirical regularities of thought processes cannot account for intention as the center of mental phenomena. We examine this issue from a reductive, behavioral perspective later.

The linguistic version of the nature of mental phenomena places intentionality as a characteristic of sentences rather than phenomena. "... A simple declarative sentence is intentional if it uses a substantival expression—a name or description—in such a way that neither the sentence nor its contradiction implies either that there is or that there isn't anything to which the substantival expression truly applies" (Chisholm, 1957, p. 170). Intentionality is absent in sentences that we use to talk about nonpsychological (physical) phenomena. We might say that the boy runs to catch the bus, but we do not say that the tree falls in order to be on the ground.

In distilling or combining the different, but equally important phenomenological and linguistic positions regarding the nature of mental activity characterized by intentionality, we may conclude the following:

1. We do not need to use intentional sentences when we describe nonpsychological phenomena. We can use physical sentences.

2. When we wish to describe perceiving, assuming, believing, knowing, wanting, hoping, and other such phenomena (Skinner's autoclitics?) then either (a) we must use intentional sentences, or (b) we must use terms we do not need to use when we describe nonpsychological phenomena. For example, "Paul drives a car" (nothing is thought by Paul), and "Lisette is French," are physical sentences. "Paul believes Lisette is French" is an example of (b).

THE BEHAVIOR ANALYSTS' POSITION

Any behavioral position is an attempt to eliminate the psychological and to express itself in physical, that is, nonintentional sentences.

Another way of saying the same thing is to say that intentional sentences are reducible to nonintentional sentences. If this can be accomplished, the intentional is eliminated, or at least translated into nonintentional terms, which potentially allows a causal analysis of mental phenomena (Ringen, 1976). This issue is at the core of theory in personality and social psychology in that its resolution will affect the way one examines the nature of human reality. The behavior analytic position maintains that when one uses the term *intention,* one is referring to the consequences a person expects will follow from a certain behavior, either in oneself or in others. It follows for the behavior analyst that an examination of intentionality as a process in human beings is a study of people's stated, expected consequences following certain behavior. There can be no mental-physical distinction regarding intentionality, as discussed earlier, as there is only human behavior and its consequences in the environment of the individual. That is, thought is verbal behavior and has an exactly similar ontological status as that of any other behavior. There is a search for functional relationships that may exist between verbal or other behavior and various environmental consequences. Skinner (1974) has summarized his position as follows:

> Evolutionary theory moved the purpose which seemed to be displayed by the human genetic endowment from antecedent design to subsequent selection by contingencies of survival. Operant theory moved the purpose which seemed to be displayed by human action from antecedent intention or plan to subsequent selection by contingencies of reinforcement. (p. 24)

Day (1976) has made the valid point that intentionality is connected with explanatory practices that give rise to the distinction between reasons for and causes of behavior. Reasons are given when an individual utilizes language to communicate information about a certain anticipated sequence of events. This may be a kind of labeling for the recognition that a certain behavior has been reinforced by certain environmental contingencies in the past and that one expects this sequence to be active in an anticipated future situation. However, to the extent that language reflects activity of the organism that cannot be attributed to a specific sequence of environmental contingencies (see chapter 5 for discussion of this point) is the extent to which reasons are fundamentally different from causes. Behavior analysts make no a priori assumptions about the particular order that may exist among these functional relationships. Therefore, the charge often levied against behavior analysts that they are mechanistic in their thinking is palpably false. Other, earlier behavioral positions, such as Hull's, did make tacit mechanistic assumptions. This lack of an a priori ontological assumption on the part of the behavior analysts places them in a strange kinship with certain aspects of phenomenology, as we shall see later. It follows that the behavior analytic position does not assume that all behavior is necessarily controlled by reinforcement (i.e., as a result of its consequences). The behavioral scientist is also assumed to be under the control of the consequences of behavior (i.e., reinforcements that are similar to those that he or she is studying). Therefore, no particular epistemology is explicitly embraced by the behavior analyst. It remains to be seen whether or not a particular epistemology or ontology is implicit in the system.

The Issue of Translation in Behavior Analysis

All verbal behavior (word utterances), the meaning of which most people and many scientists take at face, definitional value, is to be translated, according to the behavior analysts, into behavioral and reinforcement components. The meaning of words and sentences can only refer to the function that can be observed between a bit of verbal behavior and its consequences in the social environment of the subject. In addition, the behavior analyst's goal as a scientist is to have his observations increasingly influence what he says (Day, 1969). The result is that someone behaving verbally refers to an observation of some aspect of the environment that anyone can make. This verbal behavior-observation link is the same for anyone who finds him or herself in a similar situation. This, of course, allows for maximum clarity in communication. The behavior analysts are convinced that clarity is further served by translating the terms of other psychological theories into behavioral terms. This position challenges theory in personality and social psychology, and in any area particularly dependent upon explanation by verbal behavior. Decision making involving intention is keenly scrutinized.

Behavior analysts' apparent kinship with phenomenology appears with the insistence of both that phenomena (or behavior) be described as close to the observed action as possible. Both systems are descriptive and atheoretical compared with, for example, the systems of Clark Hull and Sigmund Freud.[1]

---

[1]It is important to indicate that I am comparing Freud's tripartite theory with Hull's postulate system rather than the process of psychoanalysis that inspired, among others, Maurice Merleau-Ponty in the development of his phenomenological psychology. Dollard and Miller's (1948) attempt at connecting Hull and Freud's theories is more to the point in this comparison.

This places both the radical behaviorists and the various phenome-nologists in the position of agreeing that social psychology needs to be a descriptive enterprise rather than a theoretical one—a position more or less counter to that taken by modern American social psychologists. We speak of the implications of this conclusion further on in the presentation.

The insistence by radical behaviorists that verbally expressed ideas be translated into behavioral terms brings us full circle regarding the problem of the nature of intention. If we assume for the moment that intention is a matter of verbal usage rather than an ontological issue, the radical behaviorist position closes ground with the phenomeno-logical. A person acts or behaves in order that something will happen. A frequently used summary term for this sequence is *purpose.* Behavior analysis interprets presumed purpose to be verbalized, antecedent intention that is actually reducible to subsequent selection by contin-gencies of reinforcement. Felt purpose does not have causal status in bringing about a behavior said to be intentional. Whether or not antecedent conditions have causal status or not within the context of operant theory is another issue that is discussed in some detail in chapter 5. Within this context the crucial point is that behavior analysis reinterprets felt purpose and intention as a sequence of events culmi-nating in behavior said to be felt purpose by the individual. Motives and purposes are therefore said to be the effects of reinforcement. To be aware of one's intention is to be aware of one's reinforced pattern of behavior. It follows that the behavior analytic position eschews the cause–reason distinction such as was discussed by Winch (1958), Buss (1978), and Lana (1976). Causal or contingency analysis (already dis-cussed in detail in chapter 3) is the only epistemological form of interest to the behavior analyst.

Day (1976) pointed out, however, that the idea of intention as a reason for action is frequently used by people in explaining their behavior. As this explanation is given by verbal means, it can be assumed that explicit intentions are labels for the recognition that certain behaviors are reinforced by certain contingencies. For example, Winch (1958) has written:

> Suppose that N, a university lecturer, says that he is going to cancel his next week's lectures because he intends to travel to London: here we have a statement of intention for which a reason is given. Now N does not *infer* his intention of cancelling his lectures from his desire to go London, as the imminent shattering of a glass might be inferred, either from the fact that someone had thrown a stone or from the brittleness of the glass. N does not offer his reason as *evidence* for the soundness of his prediction about his future behavior. Rather, he is justifying his intention. His statement is not of the

form: "Such and such causal factors are present, therefore this will result": nor yet of the form: "I have such and such a disposition, which will result in my doing this"; it is of the form: "In view of such and such considerations this will be a reasonable thing to do." (p. 81)

A supplementary analysis can be made that emphasizes possible contingencies or causal components in Winch's scenario. That is, even though Professor N reasons to himself in the manner proposed by Winch, he (the professor) may be passive in the face of various environmental and physiological contingencies, resulting not only in his actual behavior, but in his verbal explanation of why he behaves in the way he does. Although Professor N may not entertain a causal sequence in coming to his decision, an examination of his past life might lead one to predict the exact course of events that occurred and, also, N's articulated reasons for doing what he did. A causal analysis might have indicated a simpler, more accurate set of contingencies allowing for more accurate prediction of his behavior, verbal or otherwise.

If we reexamine Winch's example, Professor N might have argued as follows: "If I intend to go to London next week, and I most assuredly do, then I absolutely must cancel my lectures. It is physically impossible for me to be in two places at the same time and, although I would like to attend my lectures, my London trip takes precedence. I therefore do infer (i.e., it follows causally) that I cannot be at my lectures next week and in London at the same time." The impossibility of being in two places at the same time is implied by Professor N's statement of intention. The causal analysis is not superior or inferior to the intentional analysis. They are simply conceptually different and focus upon different phases of the total sequence of events described. Difficulty arises when one or the other analysis is excluded from consideration by a theorist who would explain the total sequence of events, particularly when the scenario is obviously social in nature.

Part of the program of behavior analysis concentrates on reforming language usage so that it accurately reflects the occurrence of only observable events preceding behavior that otherwise would have been labeled intentional. This position, on that account, is not incompatible with that taken by some British and continental language analysts (Chisholm, 1957).

One inescapable conclusion is that behavior analysts believe that people are verbally and therefore conceptually maladaptive in such matters as using intentional language. The sentence, "I intend to go to the movies tomorrow," implying felt purpose, would be more accurately expressed by the sentence, "I find myself anticipating certain movements that I will initiate tomorrow that will take me to the movies because I have frequently, if not always, been reinforced for these movements in the past by viewing the movie" (i.e., "It has produced a feeling in me that I call pleasure"). This sentence does not require the invocation of a concept such as intention, except as a summary noun, but instead recognizes the sequence of events that, in the past, have been reinforced in the manner indicated. The issue then turns on whether or not the phenomenological concept of intention contains references to phenomena or action of any kind that cannot be reduced to the terms of operant behavior. That is, is there any way in which an individual expressing an intention verbally escapes the contingency chain that is the basis of explanation of the behavior analysts?

A problem with the contingency explanation of intentional behavior by the behavior analysts has frequently been suggested, most recently by Rychlak (1987), that an individual can always choose to do exactly opposite of what he or she has habitually done in the past simply by so deciding. Also, knowing that someone has predicted one's behavior can result in he or she not behaving according to the prediction. Although these objections do not damage the contingency interpretation of intentional behavior in most situations, they do represent limits to its application. That is, many stated intentional acts are summaries for a sequence of environmental contingencies ending in a specified behavior. We say we are going to the butcher to buy a lamb chop because we have been previously rewarded for that behavior in the past. I suspect, however, that we produce such an intentional statement easily explained by an operant contingency analysis, because we have agreed to within the language community, not because we are in the grasp of operant contingencies. That is, we can always "step back" from our agreement that an operant analysis explains one of our intentional statements and thereby exhibit the operation of a cognitive-decisionary system that is independent of contingencies. A person may have chosen a course of action that was, indeed, reinforced; but he or she may then reject the habit out of boredom, anger, or spite. For a behavior analyst to say at that point that the person is no longer reinforced for behaving in the predicted manner is tautological.

The three concepts that have been used to explain the phenomenon of intention are the ideas of: (a) contingency and reinforcement, (b) causality, and (c) reason. Contingency and reinforcement are associated with the behavior analysts or operant reinforcers; in short, disciples of Skinner. The invocation of reason to explain intention comes from Winch, Buss, Lana, and so on, and is consistent with a general phenomenological position. The use of causation to explain intention is related to the position of the behavior analysts, but is not the same argument.

The behavior analytic position, as we have seen, assumes that intentional statements can be completely accounted for by describing a series of contiguous events involving the process of reinforcement. These contiguous events need not involve causation in the sense that an individual saying he wishes to go to the butcher to buy a lamb chop causes that act to occur because it has been reinforced in the past. The relation between cause and mere contiguity was discussed in some detail in chapter 3. Contiguous events, although they may imply causality, are not necessarily subject to it. Thus the emphasis on contiguity to explain intention is more basic to the behavior analytic argument than is the invocation of cause as a concept explaining intention. In short, a contiguous chain of events may or may not be causally determined.

Phenomenologists and others have, as we have seen, maintained that the essence of intention is contained in the nonreducible character of an individual giving a certain kind of reason why a certain sequence of behavior will follow or why one has already occurred. Further, intentional reason transcends contiguity of events as an explanatory device because it can supercede a habitual sequence as it allows for the possibility of a decision being made by the individual that is contrahabitual. This in turn, suggests that human beings are capable of making decisions that, although influenced by life contingencies, can be made freely.

None of the three concepts (cause, contingency, or reason) purporting to explain the nature of intention are necessarily contradictory to one another if all three are conceived to apply to different aspects of what is usually meant by intention. We have seen that contiguity used alone as a condition that fully explains intention faces the problem of an individual's ability to deny a prediction made on this basis once he or she simply learns of the prediction. The idea of intention as a reason given for doing something fails to consider the possibility of a previous contiguous sequence of reinforced events that might account for the reason being given (as in the Winch example). The interpretation of intention as a kind of causal sequence involving an intentional expression followed by an action of some kind suffers the same drawback and has similar virtues as the contiguity explanation.

Each of the three explanations seems to lack in convincingness what the others provide. A causal explanation requires that contiguous events be in an invariable sequence and that that sequence be related to and operate similarly to other sequences of events. (See chapter 3 for greater detail.) Giving a reason for the occurrence of an event implies that the individual is not part of a causal chain resulting in that event, but is operating independently. This further implies an ability to make decisions and affect the environment without being caused to do so by any specific causal chain of events. Again, causality implies contiguity but contiguity does not necessarily imply causality. An explanation by intent or reason implies that a cause is not operative and the contiguity of events, although discernible, is not relevant to the production of an intention.

INTENTION IN BEHAVIOR ANALYSIS
AND PHENOMENOLOGY

There is a perhaps superficial resemblance between the *weltanschauung* of the behavior analysts and that of the phenomenologists. Before we make a comparison of the two, it is important to describe some of the assumptions and observations of phenomenologists particularly regarding intention.

Phenomenology places emphasis on that which is at an opposite pole to behavior analysis. Behavior analysis is, of course, reductive in that it seeks to predict human activity in an orderly fashion by focusing on observable behavior and observable environmental conditions that are linked with it. All human activities, including what we call thought and language, are redefined to fit this contingency formula involving observable behavior and observable environmental contingencies. Speaking or thinking is behavior that can be predicted when the environmental contingencies linked to it are discovered. The behavioral scientist's explanation of human activity itself is also described in a similar vein featuring verbal behavior and preceding and following environmental contingencies.

In contrast, the phenomenologists (e.g., Husserl) begin at the other end, so to speak. Phenomenology is an "a priori psychological discipline" (Lauer, 1958, p. 34). The idea is to get beyond or behind the exclusive focus on the factual typified by many early psychologies and by current behavior analysis. It is necessary to do this precisely because a scientist is influenced by his or her indigenous human characteristics in the choice of studying the factual in the first place. Using the terms of behavior analysis, the phenomenological strategy is to describe the "behavioral repertoire" of the behavioral scientist, or, of course, of anyone. The emphasis on the a priori, much like that of behavior analysis, allows the phenomenologist to, at least temporarily, eschew the construction of theory and to concentrate on the careful description of human activity. The difference between the two systems is that behavior analysis takes the a priori as a given and concentrates on the factual through the direct observation of behavior, whereas phenomenologists concentrate on carefully describing the a priori and suspend interest in, but do not deny, the development of the factual through behavior–environment contingencies. The consequence of this difference in strategies is that the phenomenologists both assume the existence of, and use as active terms in their systems, the concepts of consciousness and intention. The world of meaning is the world of consciousness that can also be called the world of intentions. Given our discussion to this point, it comes as no surprise that phenomenologists, particularly Husserl (1960, 1964), begin their description of intentions with an analysis of language that is a product of thought. This product is assumed to be independent of any causal process and is believed to be the responses of which a human being is natively capable without specific environmental contingencies causing them.

Because the mind can signify something that may not be true, intentions cannot merely be stated, they must be verified or justified in some way. The justification or verification takes the form of what the mind signifies resting upon experience. For example, one can describe a four-footed furry animal with claws and pointed ears, but that description is devoid of meaning, which is the core of an intention, if the listener does not have a fundamental picture through perception (called an *intuition* by Husserl) ("the cat is there") or imagination ("I saw the cat in the past") of all the elements of the description. This point establishes the inseparability of intention and experience in the phenomenological position.

A person is not the outcome of various causal agencies. One is but a bit of the world. All experience, including that of a scientist, is accumulated from an individual's peculiar perspective. Science as an epistemology is secondary to phenomenal experience. To focus on things in themselves is to focus upon the world that precedes knowledge, the world of experience towards which knowledge is directed. It follows that not only science as we know it, but analytical reflections of any kind are excluded as possible methods of understanding direct experience and therefore, of understanding intentions. Analytical reflection begins with experience in the world and refers to the characteristics of the subject that are distinct from experience and that can be abstracted and summarized such as we do in science. To this extent analytical reflection is not direct experience but instead provides a reconstruction of that experience. Also, one's own reflection is aware of itself as an event. One must understand the operations of his or her own process of reflection and also recognize that this process of reflection is different from the actual event with which it is dealing. Ultimately, experiences must be described, not constructed or analyzed. This implies that perception cannot be placed into the same category as judgment, synthesis, analysis, or prediction. Perception cannot be meaningfully described probabilistically or the perceiver would not experience the perceptual stability he or she does. Perception is the background from which all acts stand out and is presupposed by them. It is possible for a person to distinguish things other than herself, as an individual does not exist as objects exist. This idea implies an acceptance of Descartes' contention embodied in the *cogitatio* that, if thought yields existence, then those entities that are imbued with the ability to think are different from those that do not have this ability. The nonthinking entities are called *things*. Before explanations of a scientific sort can be given there is plain existence, which is the stuff from which all knowledge systems evolve. The point is similar to Vico's with regard to the primacy of metaphoric language compared with logical language.

The world is what we perceive. To wonder if what we perceive is *the* world or *a* world is to already have left immediate, real experience and to have fallen back on abstraction and analysis. This position categorically removes the Humean and Kantian difficulties of wondering whether what is perceived is truly what is characteristic of the object perceived or of the individual perceiver. Phenomenologically, both objects in the world and the process of perception itself are immediately given and are not to be doubted as to their validity. The perceptual process includes the apprehension of objects in the world. They cannot be meaningfully separated. The nineteenth and twentieth century psycho-physicists spoke of illusions because they had identified certain perceptual phenomena as having a purely physical character. For example, the Muller–Lyer illusion lines are neither equal nor unequal. It is only in the objective world that this question arises. From this example, and literally hundreds more that might be cited, it is clear that the linear mensurative system is not appropriate for building expectations regarding perceptual reality. Psychologists understand this point today although they apparently did not 100 years ago.

The world is not what one thinks about, but what one lives through (Merleau-Ponty, 1962). This position also requires a rejection of the Kantian noumena-phenomena distinction discussed in chapter 3. Our relationship to the world as it appears within us is not an object that can be any further classified by a scientific or philosophical analysis. Philosophy and science can only place this relationship before us again for our perusal after it has occurred. This, by the way, is what traditional psychoanalysis does for the patient. It places an individual's relationship to the world, as he or she has lived it before him or her, without comment. Guilt and anxiety must be dealt with by the individual through his or her own phenomenological reality.

Sensation and images make their appearance within a context of meaning. An objective analysis of the nature of sensation can only be made after the individual has experienced perceptions and has considered them worthy of abstract analysis. This is a significant reversal of the Lockean and Humean idea that associations of sense impressions are the foundation of meaning. The association of sense data is yielded by experienced meaning and not the other way around. Perception inaugurates the foundation of knowledge and is not explained by it. Sense perceptions of our own body and the perception of external things are cognitively constructed determining factors external to their effects. Therefore, perception cannot be assimilated by objective thought, it can only be described.

For phenomenology, philosophy and science are suspended; they are knowledge systems, they are pursuits of the essence of experienced life. They are not attempts to deal with experienced life per se. On this assumption, it follows that the idea that human beings are the results of a series of causes is rejected. This does not mean that the idea of causation is meaningless when used to refer to human activity. It does mean, however, that there is human activity that precedes and creates the idea of cause and effect as an ontological and epistemological category. Caused, learned behavior, therefore, also cannot be primary to human existence. Human beings have the capability of abstraction, but have tended to eliminate this ability as being part of the world. That is, because they are capable of thought, human beings become confused about their own organization. They find themselves making causal conclusions about various aspects of the world and therefore conclude that they are the product of many causes. If one brackets this mode of thinking, if one discovers that he or she exists in the world immediately, moment for moment, day by day, then some of the problems that are brought about by abstraction, as how can one be both the result of a cause and the creator of one, disappear.

As we have seen, the Humean and Kantian positions lend themselves to the development of the idea that self-existence and the existence of objects other than self are doubtful. This takes the form of doubting that one can, with surety, know that a sense impression really reflects something that is true about the object of its apprehension. This doubt arises naturally enough because Kant separates, as part of his assumptions, objects in the world from self; and for Hume the individual has, in part, the same status as objects in space. Consequently, if there is some doubt about the correspondence between sense impression and the object perceived, as there frequently is, the entire process is in doubt. Avoiding this dilemma by establishing that self-processes are certain but object processes cannot be certain, Kant establishes doubt about the existence of the world outside of self. The process of doubting is a natural consequence of the separation of self from the world in the first place. In any theoretical system in psychology there are no terms, procedures, or concepts that allow one to prove or disprove one's existence. To ask someone to demonstrate existence empirically and logically is to already be in the grip of an abstract system that requires it. Another way of saying this is that when an individual believes causality to be central to understanding, he or she must deny his or her own existence because it cannot be demonstrated causally. This is abstracting ability gone berserk.

In summary, part of what the individual is, is the object it experiences. Object and experiencer are both part of the world—they ebb and flow together, they are essentially inseparable. Consequently there is no doubt about the existence of an object because there is no way that a person exists without objects (including itself). The meaning and essence of objects are described by us. What they really are is intended (given meaning) by us. We immediately know of their existence. Therefore, there is nothing that would indicate that they do not exist when we do not intend them.

Freedom

In order to be determined by external factors it is necessary that one be an object, a thing. Because human beings are perceivers and cognizer's, whereas objects external to them and parts of their bodies are not, it follows, within the phenomenological perspective, that they are free. That is, they are free to make decisions concerning themselves in the world that includes the freedom to make theories about how they are not free. There is, however, a restraint on freedom, as the initiatives of freedom itself set its limits. If I say a stream is uncrossable, this belief is set from a desire to cross it. Freedom has set a limit to its own expression. Nevertheless, this concept of freedom within the phenomenological context is distinctively different from the usually implied idea within scientific psychology that decisions made are the products of causal changes initiated in the external environment. It is not possible to prove the existence of freedom of decision or the lack of it. For the phenomemologists, it is taken as self-evident on the arguments given earlier. For determinists in general, their focus on and search for the external factors that end in behavior include a usually unstated belief in a lack of free choice.

As suggested earlier, there is a certain superficial similarity between the assumptions of behavior analysis and those of general phenomenology. Both systems purport to be atheoretical, concentrating instead upon the description of behavior (behavior analysts) or experience (phenomenologists). In short, what an organism is doing at any given moment is to be carefully described by both systems in order to gather more information about it.

Behavior analysts specify that the prediction of behavior based on organism–environment description is the desired end of their discipline. Phenomenologists describe human perception and intention in order to place themselves and others within the common experience of all. Behavior as an operative concept refers to the activities of any and all animals and plants. The experience described by phenomenologists refers only to a human beings. Since phenomenologists describe perception and intention directly, only human beings are eligible for such treatment.

Within a behavioral descriptive system, the activity of the describer is necessarily outside of the frame of reference of that which he is describing, such as, for example, the specific movements a rat makes that are followed by the appearance of food, and how this sequence is strengthened by varying the ratio of amount of food available to number of responses made. It is, of course, possible for the verbal behavior of the analyst to be described in a similar manner, but this also must be accomplished by stepping outside of the behavioral sequences being described. In short, another behavior analyst would ordinarily have to describe the behavior of an analyst analyzing. The system requires description of behavior by someone whose behavior is not then being described.

The focus of most phenomenologists is very different. Description begins with attention to one's own activities of describing. That is, the phenomenologist describes his or her own perception and intentions before being able to apply these descriptions to others, and then only tentatively. This difference between phenomenology and behavior analysis is an important distinction between systems whose assumption as to the locus of control of explanation is markedly different. Phenomenal control is internal to human beings and behavioral control is external to them.

Although these differences between the two systems are quite real, both refer to different aspects of human activity and thus are not necessarily contradictory. Historically, behavioral systems from Watson's to Skinner's have not addressed themselves to the nature of perception. Conversely, phenomenological systems have little to say about the nature of behavior change except to conclude that it succeeds rather than precedes an active decision *to* change. Behavioral systems have little to say about traditional perception because it is a phenomenon immediately experienced by the organism and can only be described as such. Perception is part of the "behavioral repertoire" of the organism and therefore enters a behavioral system only as a fact covering response possibility, not as a characteristic that can be changed by reinforcement. Conversely, behavioral change (or learning), by definition, requires the repetition (usually) of external stimuli to which an organism can react. This places behavioral change (learning) in the environment of the organism whatever its reactive capabilities, and therefore is an issue not enjoined by most phenomenologists. These clear differences in emphasis of the two systems reflect the differences in internal and external focus.

The result is that phenomenologists and behavior analysts are turned in different directions and their descriptions and explanation of human activity are supplemental to one another rather than being necessarily contradictory. To the extent that either position minimizes the importance of the other regarding the locus of control of human activity, is the degree to which they will remain incompatible.

CHAPTER 5

Skinner and the Behavior Analysts

Psychologists need little convincing that B. F. Skinner's ideas have played a seminal role in the development of psychological explanation in the 20th century. So secure is his place in the psychological firmament that his work is unhesitatingly discussed within the framework of theory as diverse as that of behavioral biology (Robinson & Woodward, 1989) and social psychology. The widespread applicability of the questions he raises is a clue to the fact that Skinner's thinking is fundamentally epistemological. As early as 1953 in *Science and Human Behavior* Skinner was concerned with the predictability of behavior and the issue of whether human beings can freely choose various courses of action. Consequently, one of the core issues with which Skinner was concerned was how we come to know what we know. In one sense, which hopefully becomes apparent as this chapter unfolds, most of the questions he raises and attempts to answer are epistemological to a greater degree than almost any other psychological theorist of this century. It is this epistemological bent that makes Skinner's work so important to every area of psychology.

The form that Skinner's epistemology takes is uncomplicated, cleanly empirical, and a direct descendant of ideas that English-speaking people have found compatible since the days of the British empiricists. Skinner's propositions about the nature of human existence and how we may come to know that nature are distinctly different from most other psychological views from Freud's heyday to today. This chapter focuses on what Skinner has to say about those situations that involve one individual reacting to another usually through language or through other symbols.

79

WHAT SKINNER ASSERTS

Much has been written, both by Skinner and by his associates, about the core of beliefs and techniques used in their building explanation of various aspects of human activity, and it is crucial that those beliefs be reiterated as assumptions for the discussion that follows.

Behaviorism refers to the ideas of the earliest theorists, principally John Watson. No clear distinction is made between these ideas and those of the so-called neobehaviorists who utilize mediational concepts anchored by operational definitions. Skinner has called the latter approach, "methodological behaviorism." Nonmediational, environment-based accounts of behavior are part of the behavior-analytic (Skinnerian) approach to explanation. This is also occasionally called "radical behaviorism." Behavior analysis accepts the idea that some human events are private to the individual, but are not thereby different from overt behavior.

Although some neobehaviorists (e.g., Spence, 1956) make a distinction between behaviorism and neobehaviorism, the difference is not important to analytic behaviorists. Typically, behavior analysts contrast their position with that of neobehaviorists and other theoretical positions that utilize mediational concepts (e.g., Freud, 1960).

The most troublesome mediational explanatory concepts for the behavior analysts are those involving thought, ideas, or cognitions, particularly when invoked to explain some observable behavior that is a presumed effect following a mental cause such as an intention, desire, or decision. The behavior analyst eschews the use of "mentalistic" concepts in the explanation of human activity. By so doing, behavior analysts believe they have finally settled the centuries old dualism of mind and body that has been preserved well into the twentieth century.

The rejection of mediational concepts places the behavior analysts in the position of eliminating many formerly perplexing problems addressed by earlier theorists. Their system attempts to answer the fundamental question: What are the arrangements of organism and environment that are useful for predicting what the organism will do at any given time? What we call thinking is no different, for predictive purposes, than any other behavior such as eating, walking, etc. By making all human responses the same in terms of their potential for being linked with other behavior or objects and events in the environment, the idea of thought or ideas giving rise to, or causing a physical action, cannot arise as an explanatory possibility. All dualisms from the Greeks through Descartes and those implied in the impression–idea dualism of the British associationists are eliminated.

Noumena–phenomena distinctions are likewise laid to rest because the behavior analysts implicitly assume that objects, events, or persons exist if they can enter an observable sequence that ends in some bit of behavior. The ontological acceptance of objects is tacit. Behavior for the behavior-analyst is, as we have seen, analogous to experience for the phenomenologist. The behavior-analysis position is enlarged by the acceptance of private events as behaviors to be analyzed no differently from any other behavior, although they are not observable by other than the behaving individual. It is very difficult to hide that behavior we label "running." If one is running someone can, at least potentially, see her running. If, however, one is thinking about going to the beach, no one can observe that behavior even in the presence of the individual doing the thinking. That private thought, however, can enter into a sequence of observable behaviors that actually allows one to observe the individual going to the beach. Thought that is communicable always involves language, thus the nature of language acquisition and use is crucial to the behavior analysts, and we deal with this in the following pages.

By accepting private events as behaviors no different from any other, the behavior analysts may then include what is ordinarily labeled "thought" as verbal behavior that is not uttered. These behaviors constitute the active life of an organism. The behaviors are different from time to time in any one organism and different from one organism to another because they are different in their consequences. These consequences reinforce the behavior preceding them and hence increase the probability of those behaviors occurring under similar environmental and organismic conditions in the future. A consequence is positively reinforcing if the probability of the occurrence of the response that precedes it is increased. Behaviors are eliminated if those behaviors are followed by consequences that decrease the likelihood of their occurring in the future. If these definitions sound circular, they are, but the circularity disappears if an observer is introduced into the cycle.

When an animal periodically presses a bar such that a small amount of food is released into a cup, followed by the animal eating the food, an observer may legitimately conclude that the succeeding increased number of bar presses per unit of time is somehow connected to the animal consuming a small amount of grain. If the feeder mechanism is adjusted so that no matter how often the animal presses the bar, no grain falls into the cup, it can be observed that the animal eventually stops the behavior of bar pressing. That is, behavior and its consequences can be seen as a single unit with two parts. As it is possible for us to disrupt the unit by manipulating a part of it (the consequence of a behavior) and thereby effect the behavior, no inherent circularity is involved in the concepts of reinforcement, behavior, and consequence. A human being can make the same observation about his or her own behavior. That is, I can observe that when I have not eaten for several hours, my behavior brings me into contact with food, which I then consume. I can observe that my behavior of food seeking (e.g., going to a restaurant) is reinforced by the food I receive there. The lack of circularity is apparent from my observation that my explaining this food-seeking behavior to myself in no way either precipitated the behavior, nor particularly interrupts it once I have made my analysis. That is, I can notice my food-seeking behavior being reinforced. Of course, having made my analysis, I can then modify my behavior, but that is another issue discussed later.

The issue of circularity is enjoined by the issue of causality as it is used by behavior analysts. As we have seen, all those who have discussed causation in the past, from Hume and Kant to current analysts, separate the issue into its epistemological and ontological components. The behavior analysts do not.

CAUSATION AND THE BEHAVIOR ANALYSTS

It is clear that the behavior analyst position does not explicitly sub-scribe to the interpretation of causation of either that of Hume or of Kant. Both Hume and Kant require that the nature of causation be ascribed to a way of interpreting the world that is indigenous to human beings and that involves objects of perception, but not necessarily objects as they exist in the external world. Causation for both Hume and Kant, but for Kant more explicitly, is a conclusion (A causes B necessarily) that people reach in order to differentiate their perception of mere sequential order (contiguity of perceived objects in space and time) from their perception of sequential order of events, one of which necessarily follows the other. As we have seen, this interpretation is clearly epistemological while skirting the ontological character of causation.

Because the focus of behavior analysis is on an event, whether it is an object perceived in space or a private perception (thought) linked with a consequent, there is a tacit acknowledgment of a noumenal world and discussion of the indigenous nature of the inferrer that allows that an inference of cause to effect is eliminated. Yet behavior analysts (e.g., Day, 1976) speak of causation within behavioral theory. There are at least two possibilities for interpreting the meaning of causation within the system: (a) causation as a highly probable, but not invariable, sequence of observed events to others involving no other assumptions, or (b) a highly probable sequence of succeeding events yielding a functional relationship between two or more variables, this relationship constituting the idea of necessity as described in the section in chapter 3 on a modern conception of causality.

Causation and contiguity

The idea of causation is a concept the behavior-analysts do not usually care to embrace (cf. Hineline, 1990; Hineline & Wanchisen, 1989). Indeed, it is not necessary for most scientists to address the issue of causality so long as they pursue their successful research that leads to useful practicalities. However, psychologists generally do not have that luxury as part of their job is to explore the very nature of scientific as well as others forms of behavior.

The legitimacy of inferring causally is not usually discussed by behavior-analysts even though they do infer causally. The tacit position taken is that frequently occurring observable behaviors and consequences can be taken as a basis for expecting the occurrence of the behavior in the future if certain conditions in the environment are sufficiently similar to previous occasions. This expectancy is useful for successfully dealing with various aspects of life. No question is raised as to why such an observed arrangement is practical or why the inferrer can legitimately infer a consequence in an unobserved time (the future). The physicist can avoid this curiosity without damage to his mode of explanation; the psychologist cannot. If the behavior-analyst were to accept the Hume-Kant solutions involving the assignment of proclivities to the organism not reducible to behavior and consequent sequences, then he or she would be acknowledging a semi-independent (not dependent on a specifiable sequence of events) private process in human beings, and perhaps animals, which they would like to avoid within their own explanatory context.

They can, however, maintain a position of neutrality regarding the issue of the nature of the legitimacy of causal inference, as suggested previously, and simply declare that causal inferring is useful whatever its basis. This position, of course, leaves the behavior of causal inference unaccounted for by the behavior analysts.

Necessity and the Behavior Analysts

Let us assume behavior analysts will accept the idea that contiguity of behavioral and environmental events must be present as a condition for making a prediction in the future regarding the appearance of the behavior in question. Further, the success of each succeeding prediction adds an increment to the solidity of the belief that the observer can truly predict appropriate behavior in the future, at least to some asymptote of belief that will not increase with further successful predictions.

In order to establish a truly causative relationship in the sequence of events leading to successful prediction, it is necessary that the behavior analyst show (a) the relation that holds among any series of similar predictions, and (b) the relationship that holds among related general predictive statements. The ability to show irrefutable links between classes of predictive statements would then establish the necessity of the effect (behavior) following a cause (consequence and or previous behavior). With this in mind it is necessary to locate such related predictive statements within the behavior analytic enterprise.

Schedules of reinforcement developed more or less continuously over the past 50 years provide us with such statements. An early collection of these generalized predictions are, of course, presented in Ferster and Skinner's (1957) *Schedules of Reinforcement.* Thirteen schedules of reinforcement are presented by the authors, although there are four basic types: (a) fixed ratio, (b) variable ratio, (c) fixed interval, and (d) variable interval.

The fixed ratio schedule consists of a reinforcement appearing upon the completion of a fixed number of responses made by the organism. The variable-ratio schedule requires that a response be reinforced according to a random series of ratios, the mean of which is set by the experimenter. For example, the second response given by the organism might be reinforced, then the fourth response after that, etc., with the mean ratio being set at three responses. Fixed interval reinforcement is one in which responses are reinforced at a given time interval; that is, a response is reinforced when it is made after a certain amount of time has elapsed since the last reinforced response. In variable interval reinforcement, responses are reinforced according to a series of random time intervals (3 seconds, then 5 seconds, etc.) with a preset mean.

Over a number of years, many experiments have been performed where pecking in pigeons and bar pressing in rats were studied in order to determine development and changes in these responses. The result was a series of two-dimensional functional curves that describe this activity. A typical fixed ratio function is shown in Fig. 5.1. An experiment begins with the animal being continuously reinforced; that is, it receives food every time it makes the appropriate response. After the rate of responding has begun to level off, the fixed ratio is introduced and rate of responding increases over time to a maximum. Should the fixed ratio be either increased or lowered, the resulting functional

FIG. 5.1. Responses to fixed ratio reinforcement. Stylized plot of the transition from continuous reinforcement to fixed ratio reinforcement. The arrow indicates the onset of fixed ratio reinforcement. (After Figure 12 p. 42, Skinner & Ferster, 1957.)

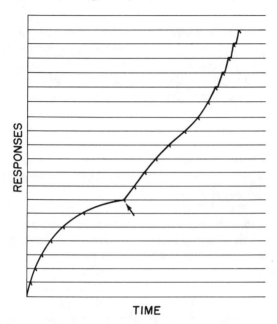

TIME

relationship between rate of responding and that ratio will have a proportional value to the previous ratio. For example, if a ratio is changed and then changed again, the rate of responding will generate three different curves. Because the three functions that have been generated are predictably related to one another quantitatively, prediction of an animal's behavior under any one of the fixed ratios can be said to be a causal statement because of the relationship among the empirically determined functions. If only one fixed ratio resulted in the ability to predict the reinforcement behavior sequence, and no other ratios allowed for consistent prediction, then we would suspect the causal efficacy of the one fixed ratio that did work. That is, our expectation of fixed ratios of reinforcement affecting behavior would not be increased. Instead we might suspect that the one fixed ratio that allowed for successful prediction was an anomaly or described merely contiguous events that required further study. In addition, the fixed ratio functions can be shown to be related quantitatively to fixed interval functions as the time it takes an animal to respond in the fixed ratio situation is directly related to time as a significant condition in the fixed interval reinforcement procedure that has generated its own empirical function.

Consequently there are two quantitative relationships existing within the conclusions drawn by behavior analysis; the quantitative relations of responses within one of the reinforcement types (e.g., fixed ratio) and between the reinforcement types (e.g., fixed ratio and fixed interval). These results meet the criteria of necessity in causal statements along with the criterion of constant conjunction between the cause and effect. I therefore conclude that the behavior analysis position does indeed tacitly hold to the epistemological conclusion that the sequence, behavior-consequence-behavior-consequence, etc., is a causative sequence. That is, it adds an increment of understanding to believe that this sequence of behavior and consequence is not merely a set of contiguous observations, but is something beyond that in that it changes the behavior of the behavior analyst (his or her belief) in the efficacy of the prediction being made and therefore also in the efficacy of the causal principal underlying it.

Often the charge is leveled at behavior analysts that they believe that animals and human beings are "mechanical" or that their activity is to be explained by developing a set of mechanical causative sequences that will fully describe them with no loss of meaning. Mechanical causation requires that the events that are to be identified as causes and effects be in physical contact with one another. For example, if a billiard ball resting on a table is to move at all it must be struck or touched by another object in motion. The resulting motion of the billiard ball is said to be caused by a body in motion touching it. Within a biopsychological context, an electric current passing through a wire that is touched to the rear leg of a dog is said to be the cause of the dog's leg moving quickly away from the wire. In both cases the causal sequence is said to be mechanical. Also, in both cases other laws and principles may be invoked, such as Newton's laws of motion and laws associated with nerve impulse conduction respectively, to explain the mechanical causation noted.

It is clear that the sequence of response-consequence-response, etc., need not be mechanical as a consequence such as the consumption of a pellet of food that has fallen into a cup is not a behavior that is physically connected with the behavior of pressing a bar. Also, an animal removed from such a situation will eventually continue bar pressing at a different rate from one not previously so exposed. This indicates that the sequence of bar press-eating–bar press, etc., cannot represent a mechanical causal sequence. This does *not* mean that an analogy of animals as machines is one that must be eschewed by behavior analysts, should they choose to use it. There are machines that operate mechanically and those that operate in some other manner, for example, electronically.

Causation as an Ontological Characteristic

What remains is to determine whether or not the behavior analyst position is implicitly ontological with respect to its tacit acceptance of causation as a process that is separate from, but which underlies, the nature of the theory as discussed earlier.

The very fact that there are behavior analytic laws that are reasonably consistent, such as the "law of fixed ratios," the "law of fixed intervals," etc., which are themselves logically connected by principles other than those of the behavior analytic system itself (i.e., by the rules of logic), indicates that behavior analysis is fundamentally ontologic regarding the acceptance of the causal principle. The derivations that can he made from what I will call the "law of the fixed ratio" further tests the nature of reality. This is expressed in the ability of behavior analysts to make more correct predictions regarding reinforced behavior. Ultimately, it does not matter whether the law of the fixed ratio is true or not, or even whether or not behavior-analyst predictions are successful, in whether or not they tacitly accept the ontological reality of the causal principle. The manner in which the system gathers its information and makes its conclusions requires this belief.

The logic of behavior analysis is consistent with and, indeed, requires an acceptance of not only the Humean perspective on the nature of causality, but the Kantian one as well. This tacit acceptance of the Hume–Kant position, however, establishes only their epistemological position with regard to causation. The ontological acceptance of the causal principle is also established by accepting the idea that the general principles of behavior analysis, such as are expressed in the prediction of behavior via various schedules of reinforcement, are useful because they are connectable by concepts not part of the terms of the system itself.

Most likely the behavior-analyst reaction to the idea that the principles of connection of the terms of their system are not part of that system would produce disagreement. The disagreement would most likely take the form of an argument that the principles of logic, induction, and deduction used by the behavior-analyst, although not part of the system he or she is constructing, are analyzable in the same terms. In short, the ideas of logic are verbally or symbolically expressed and that verbal or symbolic activity is behavior and therefore amenable to examination in the same manner as any behavioral system. To his credit, Skinner not only accepted this notion, but attempted to show how that analysis might be accomplished in *Verbal Behavior* (1957), which will be discussed later.

Having concluded that behavior analysis necessarily accepts causation as both an epistemological and an ontological truth, I find it possible to present another, noncontradictory possibility. If causality is a fundamentally ontological characteristic, then in order for an explanation to be causal, the entire process of origination or of production must exist outside of the object concerned. That is, if an object is in any way caused to do anything or change in any way as a necessary result of some activity, this activity must not be part of the action that the object itself can initiate. From this conception of causation, which is totally ontological, the behavior analysts must consider that the analysis of behavior–environment sequences is necessarily incomplete and that another tact must be taken to complete or to extend analysis. Behavior analysts hold that an organism can be active and contribute to, and interact with, other aspects of its environment when behavior is forthcoming. Later we see that the autoclitic as a concept in Skinner's analysis of verbal behavior is fundamentally noncausal and thus represents an important instance of an explanatory concept that is outside of the usual framework of what is meant by an effect being caused.

So far as the behavior analysts themselves are concerned, to the extent that there are laws of behavior (fixed ratio, fixed interval, etc.) I suggest that causality as an aspect of natural arrangements involving behavior is ontologically acceptable.

Does it matter what the behavior analyst position is with regard to these various conceptions of causation? I believe it does, as part of the subject matter of any attempt at a complete psychology, which behavior analysis seeks to be, is to explain the nature of the processes involved in making explanations, that is, what we call thought, reasoning, logic, etc. This in turn requires that verbal behavior be carefully examined as it is the vehicle of human attempts at explanation. Further, because verbal activity is inherently social (a means of communication with others), the results of this examination will have serious implications for our ability to deal with social activity.

ANALYSIS OF VERBAL BEHAVIOR

When people speak to one another they produce a form of behavior. No other concepts such as "social" or "thought" need to be utilized in order to predict and explain this activity. Speech is verbal behavior and thought is an individual speaking to herself. In contrast to this Skinnerian, behavior analytic position, is the idea that words have meaning beyond their behavior consequences, or that there is information conveyed by words independent of their behavioral consequences.

Behavior analysis attempts to describe the sequence of observable events in behavioral and reinforcement terms to discover the meaning of meaning. No experimental results are used to support conclusions, thus Skinner's description of verbal behavior is in the form of a hermeneutic analysis of the text of ordinary speech. This analysis, however, is not of the usual kind of analyzing the meaning and context of words, but of reducing these presumed meanings to reinforcement contingencies associated with verbal behavior.

The models used to cast verbal behavior in a causal form are those that have previously been developed from experimental work on nonverbal behavior. Thus, the meaning of words is a property of the conditions under which verbal behavior occurs.

The Verbal Operants

Skinner classified language usage into several different verbal operants. The *mand* is a verbal command in which the response is reinforced by a repeated consequence under the functional control of a relevant condition of deprivation or aversive stimulation. That is, hearing the mand, "Wait!", is followed by aversive stimulation if the listener does not, indeed, wait. The form of the word alone, however, will not necessarily allow one to correctly conclude that a verbal utterance is a mand. Being familiar with the verbal community in which the mand is used is necessary to make this determination.

A *magical mand* is defined as verbal behavior that has a command implied but that could not have been reinforced at any time. Utterances such as, "Be alive, Shakespeare," are as mundane as demanding an object one has never received as reinforcement before when uttering a mand such as "Give me all your money." The speaker creates these, Skinner claims, by analogy to reinforced mands in his or her repertoire. The implication is that the speaker has the nonreinforced ability to generalize from one situation to a similar situation, which has involved reinforcement. Skinner includes the ability to make analogies and to generalize from one situation to another in verbal behavior even though these abilities are, by definition, not developed themselves by reinforcement.

A *tact,* as in "makes contact with," is a verbal operant in which a response is evoked or strengthened by a particular object or event or property of an object or event. Again, as with the mand, the verbal community determines what verbal responses are tacts. If a person points to a red object and pronounces, "red," which is followed by a listener saying, "Right," the speaker is reinforced in using the verbal operant "red" in the future when confronted by a similar object, by the reinforcement of the listener having said "Right." Generally, a tact extends the contact of the listener to his or her environment. It allows the listener to act as a speaker of tacts that extends the contact to the environment of other listeners. Reinforcement is in the form of an object or event or some part of an object or event, reinforcing the tacting behavior of both the speaker and the listener. Skinner discusses these sequences of reinforcement and behavior in detail in *Verbal Behavior* (pp. 84–85).

Skinner also classified other forms of verbal behavior into categories such as *echoic response, textual,* and *interverbal behavior.* In all of these, the response is controlled by various aspects of the environment or by the past reinforcement history of the organism. The situation where the speaker him or herself is the director and organizer of verbal behavior produces such responses as "if," "that," "before," "I guess," "I esti-mate," "I believe," "I concede," and "I infer." This class of response Skinner called *autoclitic.* He argued that autoclitics, in which the atten-dant reinforcement contingencies are not as obvious as they are in other forms of verbal behavior, are derivative from the forms of verbal responses that are subject to such reinforcements. Grammar and syntax are considered to be autoclitic processes. This form of verbal response, where the speaker *seems* to be in control, is associated with what most of us call thinking, logic, and various creative acts. Skinner stated:

> There are at least two systems of responses, one based upon the other. The upper level can only be understood in terms of its relations to the lower. The notion of an inner self is an effort to represent the fact that when behavior is compounded in this way, the upper system seems to guide or alter the lower. But the controlling system is itself also behavior. The speaker may, "know what he is saying" in the sense in which he "knows" any part or feature of the environment. Some of his behavior (the "known") serves as a variable in control of other parts ("knowing"). Such "propositional attitudes" as asser-tion, negation, quantification, the design achieved through reviewing and rejecting or emitting responses, the generation of quantities of verbal be-havior merely as such, and the highly complex manipulations of verbal thinking can all, as we shall see, be analyzed in terms of behavior which is evoked by or acts upon other behavior of the speaker. (1957, p. 313)

What are the alternatives to Skinner's autoclitic for explaining these complex verbal processes? Whether they be presented by Chomsky (1966), or Brentano (1973, modern edition) in the last century, or any other semanticist-syntacticalist, counterarguments generally empha-size the idea that human beings are capable of verbal invention that is not necessarily linked to identifiable chains of past verbal behavior and reinforcement. Presumably the ever-active human brain is capable of making responses that, although cast in a form (language) that most accept as learned, are also produced by inherent brain activity. That is, the position can be taken that the structure of the human brain determines its function, which is thought expressed in language. The functions of other parts of the body are similarly determined. For example, if I ask why the human arm bends (behaves) only in one direction when it bends at all, a satisfying answer is that it is structured so that the ball-in-socket joint at the elbow physically restrains the forearm when it moves in one direction but not when it moves in the opposite direction. We are convinced that this is a reasonable explanation when we actually examine the human bones in that part of the arm either by X-ray or by looking at a human skeleton. *When* the arm will bend in the one direction that it can bend, we accept, is a question better answered by referring to a reinforcement schedule. However, we need to know the structural reality to complete the analysis to our satisfaction. Applying this analogy to human brain function regarding language is different in focus than, and extends, a thoroughly behavioral analysis.

The counterpart to examining the actual structure of the arm is either to examine the actual structure of the brain that produces verbal behavior, which we cannot do now to any degree that informs us as to the nature of verbal behavior, or to use an intermediate step in the process of building an explanation. That step is to assume that the brain's structure is consistent with its operation and to describe that operation (thought, verbal behavior) by reference to its form. This is precisely what Chomsky has attempted to do. The main point of that analysis, for our purpose, is that thought is said to create ideas that are independent of any *specific* chain of reinforcing events. As we have seen from our discussion of phenomenology in chapter 4, these ideas, however, are not independent of events in the world.

If we return to Skinner's idea of the autoclitic, we can progress further regarding the nature of intention as discussed in chapter 4. In addition, the idea of causation within the behavior analytic position changes when verbal behavior and especially the autoclitic are discussed.

In *Verbal Behavior* and elsewhere, Skinner used the term *causation* or *cause,* and spoke of *multiple causation,* and so on, so that there is little doubt that he subscribed to some idea of causation. We have seen at the beginning of this chapter that, given the structure of behavior analytic theory regarding the various schedules of reinforcement, the system requires an ontological belief in causation. When we reach discussion of verbal behavior, however, the causative waters become muddied. A series of schedules of reinforcement involving verbal behavior would, of course, be soundly consistent with the implicit position of the behavior analysts regarding an ontic belief in causation. However, no such schedules are presented regarding verbal behavior. The reason is, of course, that no meaningful experiments regarding the acquisition and use of language as a product of reinforcement have been performed. This is understandable since experimentation would require the control of young children just learning language and this is not ethically or practically possible. Skinner instead described language behavior so as to produce a series of explanations about acquisition and use that are feasible, if not directly demonstrable. The analysis is ex post facto, but then virtually all language analysis of acquisition and use is, except for studies done on general language development in children.

Even with this nonexperimental approach to language, Skinner clearly intended that the form of his explanation be no different than that offered regarding schedules of reinforcements discovered in animals and discussed earlier in this chapter. If the autoclitic system is one in which some verbal behavior reinforces other verbal behavior, the causal chain suggested by events external to the organism reinforcing behavior is broken. That is, causality cannot mean, ontologically, that an individual has control over his or her behavior, however described. Such an organism may still be described by analogy to a machine, but the autoclitic must be outside of the idea of causality as an ontological condition. Causality as an epistemological characteristic of human explanations is not disturbed by the autoclitic because the autoclitic is a description of the way humans think (or behave when we call that behavior "thinking"). However, because the autoclitic is a concept that describes behavior (i.e., behavior influencing behavior) it involves only verbal internal processes and therefore is different from those explanations of behavior when the reinforcement is clearly external to the organism such as is found in predictions from fixed ratio or fixed interval laws.

The separation of the autoclitic as an explanatory concept from other behavior analytic concepts is further demonstrated by the fact that there are predictive laws developed for externally reinforced behavior, but not for autoclitic behavior that is dealt with ex post facto. Other forms of verbal behavior such as the mand or tact, being subject to clearly defined external reinforcement, can, in theory, have predictive schedules of reinforcement applied to them.

I suspect that behavior analysts will not accept this argument on the assumption that the sequence of behavior-behavior-external reinforcement that is part of the process whereby an autoclitic is formed, can be, at least theoretically, shown to be part of a causal chain no different from that implied in, for example, a fixed ratio schedule or any other schedule of reinforcement. However, the burden of proof is on the behavior-analyst regarding either what ontic causation asserts or, barring that, what they mean by causation when they use the term if it is not ontic. It could be that the behavior analysts hold that causation is used simply to refer to the contiguous arrangement of events that include reinforcements and behavior and that alone. This position, however, as we have seen, would belie the clear ontic character causation is given in the various laws expressed by schedules of reinforcement.

Perhaps Skinner himself has indicated the path of resolution of this problem regarding the autoclitic in his chapter on thinking. He said: "All behavior, verbal or otherwise, is subject to Kantian a priori's in the sense that man as a behaving system has inescapable characteristics and limitations" (p. 451).

It is these inescapable characteristics and limitations that were briefly described, in form, in the example given previously of the functional analysis of thought as a "brain working" compared with a functional analysis of "arm working" in a certain way and not another because of the structure of both. Chomsky's analysis of deep structure is an instance of describing characteristics and limitations of thought that are implied in the Kantian imperative. This approach need not be contradictory to an analysis of verbal behavior if it is accepted that those behaviors implied by the autoclitic may be ascribable more to the Kantian characteristics and limitations of human thought than they are ascribable to a causal chain of events involving external reinforcement accompanying behavior.

Neither the behavioral nor the structural explanations of complex thought exclude the idea of thinking or autoclitic behavior as part of a machine analogy. Both points of view can be taken as descriptions of a working human machine. Indeed, except in the case where one invokes a sentient, interested God, no other analogue is possible on the assumption that human beings are products of their DNA molecules and are, in that sense, completely determined in everything they are and in everything they *can* do. (*Can* do, not *will* do.) The job of the psychologist is to describe human possibilities for behavior including thought or, if you will, verbal behavior. Modern psychologists attribute no magical qualities to the ability of human beings to generate ideas, thoughts, or behavior of other kinds that are not themselves subject to analysis regarding their source. The question is where to look and how to describe those sources. Skinner and the behavior analysts' insistence on analyzing only behavior as both the source and substance of understanding human existence is both reasonable and, at least nowadays, truistic. At the turn of the century, the idea was radical, as it was perhaps 50 years ago. Today, most psychologists accept behavior as the focal point of their efforts. However, as we have seen previously there is more than one way to go about it. In this sense Chomsky is as much focused on behavior as is Skinner. The crux of the issue seems to turn on whether the organism always behaves as a result of specific reinforcement or whether he or she is capable of reacting from simple contact with the world.

SOCIAL BEHAVIOR

In 1953 Skinner defined *social behavior* as, ". . . the behavior of two or more people with respect to one another or in concert with respect to a common environment" (p. 297). He also said that nothing unique arises in social activity such as "social forces" or "social situations" that cannot be described in the language of natural science. No social psychologist, at least since World War II, would disagree so long as natural science is broadened beyond the confines of experimental science. Skinner's description of social behavior requires, as one might expect, heavy dependence on communication via language (verbal behavior). That is, verbal behavior always requires social reinforcement. A person asking for a glass of water, Skinner pointed out, would have no effect on any part of the environment other than another individual. Consequently, Skinner's arguments regarding the description of social behavior is only as solid as the accuracy of his description of verbal behavior. We have already expressed some doubts about the total adequacy of that description, thus, it will be more fruitful to move on to another aspect of the behavior analytic approach to describing social behavior.

In examining various social episodes and describing them in the terms of the reinforcement of behavior in a similar fashion to that applied to individual behavior, Skinner further suggested that social scientists may not necessarily state their generalizations in terms of individual behavior ". . . since another level of description may also be valid and may well be more convenient" (1953, p. 298). As most psychologists are thoroughly familiar with Skinner's analysis of social behavior as set forth in *Science and Human Behavior,* it interests me more to examine the implications of this last statement than to pursue the application of behavioral analysis to social activity.

Why are levels of description other than the behavioral more convenient? If I am curious about why a group of Americans behave in certain ways I might find that the written laws of the group (prescriptions for behavior) are mainly derived from the written, more general prescriptions in the U.S. Constitution. By examining it, I might find that the laws today cohere to a few ideas written in this document. I then conclude that the idea, "that all men are created equal," is the behavioral suggestion that has lead to the specific laws in which I am interested. If I ask in turn how I am to describe the reinforcement contingencies that lead to these behavioral prescriptions in the Constitution, I would be at a considerable loss because it was written 200 years ago. Consequently, I have only the behavioral "prescription" or the "meaning" of the words in the Constitution to enlighten me. This means that I must take the meaning of the words seriously if I am to be able to predict certain behavior today. This analysis does not contradict behavior analysis, but it does require a shift in methodology from direct behavior analysis to an analysis of written record. It is not merely more convenient to do so, as Skinner suggests, it is an absolute necessity if we are to understand the reinforcement history of a group of people living together.

If I were curious as to why a son or daughter is given the last name of the father (patronym) in addition to a first name that may or may not be unique in that family, the only answer that is suitable is sociohistorical. It is clear that an extended family has many patronyms associated with it, thus it should also be clear that simply adding one to another and assigning them to a newborn, would soon prove unwieldy and impractical. Some groups, the Spanish for example, do carry several last names, both patronyms and matronyms, forward, but for reasons of practicality, use fewer than are assigned. The current occasional American practice of assigning both the mother and father's last names to a child would also soon prove impractical with the next generation. It is clear that only one surname has to be assigned to a child if the system is to remain consistent. Of course, this could be the mother's last name instead of the father's. An analysis of the consequence of naming behavior can be made in terms of the legal necessity of having a family name because of the laws of inheritance, responsibility for minors, etc. However, as already stated, these laws would themselves have to be analyzed historically. Vico explained the relevant history as follows:

In the early days of Rome, the general populations of plebeians were brought under the control of the nobles by their agreement to serve them for the protection the nobles afforded. These plebeians were virtual slaves and were not allowed to marry nor carry patronyms other than those of the noble overlord. Marriage, and therefore the identification of the patronym, was denied the plebeians and became in itself a mark of nobility. The plebeians were totally in bail to their lords. After much travail and open revolution, the plebeians demanded and received the rights of the auspices especially regarding marriage (connubium). When this demand was met by the nobles, the plebeians had effectively ceased to be slaves and became citizens.

When a son may take his father's name, it paves the way for his taking his property also, and thus he gains the right to have his actions judged by the same laws as those existing for the nobles (Vico, 1961, modern edition). Obviously, women stood very differently than men in relation to these laws, but that is another story.

As in the previous analysis, this sociohistorical one is certainly not contradictory to a behavior analysis, but again as in the example involving the U.S. Constitution, the shift in our explanatory emphasis is more than just a matter of convenience. The sociohistoric can be said to be a record of the behavior and reinforcement context that allows us to predict specific behaviors today of groups of people in their reactions to various social stimuli in their environments. It is possible to conclude that a person both says that he believes all people should have equal access to work and behaves consistent with that belief because he is currently reinforced for those beliefs and behaviors. It is also possible to conclude that the history of the beliefs involved give one as much information regarding the individual's behavior as the individual behavioral assessment. To insist on a behavioral assessment to predict some social behavior, such as that indicated, is cumbersome even though one might accept that reinforcement is involved. In addition, if we consider a person's belief in the validity of a particular behavioral reinforcing system that involves social behavior, then another layer of behavior and reinforcement is involved. That is, people believe certain things about social context that may or may not be coherent and useful for prediction, but that, nevertheless, constitutes an active system by which they live. For example, one may believe that there is a powerful, caring entity called God who is concerned about one's life and therefore lives their life differently than one's fellow who does not believe in such a God. As we have seen historically, various patterns of social reinforcement develop that affect everyday behavior differentially when such groups of people live within the jurisdiction of the same political entity or even when they are oceans apart. Clearly this fact requires an epistemology to handle these problems that is different from individual behavioral analysis. This different behavioral epistemology is *not* reducible to that of the analysis of individual behavior because it is both historical and involves peoples' belief systems that are directed toward their own patterns of reinforced behavior. The result is a need for a multilevel epistemological system.

The examination of individual reinforced behavior requires the bracketing of the sociohistorical facts that are relevant to that particular individual reinforcement history. Conversely, individual reinforcement history is bracketed when examining a sociohistorical belief system. The analyses need not be contradictory, but they do represent different epistemologies.

Vico's distinction between certum and verum, and his idea that a "new science" was needed to deal with human beings as they live in groups was not the natural science that Descartes had envisioned. It was a science attuned to the universal history of the group.

People believe many things about their own nature and about the nature of the world around them. These beliefs do not always coincide with the beliefs of scientists who study people. People's errors regarding phenomena of which there are generally accepted (by the scientific community) alternative correct beliefs, are in themselves interesting. Those erroneous beliefs, as well as those on which most everyone agrees, constitute, in part, the subject matter of social psychology and must be examined for their own internal logic and context.

This is not to suggest that something emerges that is "the social," which lies beyond people behaving. Rather, it suggests that there are better ways than behavioral analysis to study people's behavior in groups (e.g., the sociohistorical as illustrated previously). With this, it is still possible to assume that reinforced behavior is always involved in what people actually do. What does "emerge" is a diverse epistemology, although not a different ontology, that separates individual from social behavior.

Let me be clear that I am not referring to methodological differences alone between behavior analysis and a social analysis, but fundamental, epistemological, although not necessarily ontological differences between the two approaches. In short, the methods of sociohistorical epistemology cannot be reduced to behavior analytic methods nor the other way around, based on the essentially Vichean arguments presented earlier. The difference between the two is as profound as the difference between the epistemology of Newtonian physics and that of quantum mechanics.

There is a social community into which the individual is born and by which the individual is influenced in many of his or her behaviors. In addition, and operating simultaneously with social influence, is the personal idiosyncratic reinforcement history of the individual that develops his or her response patterns in not only social, but other situations as well. Most children may be reinforced for saluting the national flag by their teacher's approval. At the same time, one individual may be reinforced with fried zucchini for reciting one's prayers in Latin, although this experience is shared by very few other people within the social group.

If both the individual who is the subject of our focus and we as observers are interested in predicting behavior, or placing it as a product within a coherent conceptual scheme that explains the phenomena to our satisfaction, we are dealing with epistemological issues that require a different sort of scrutiny than that provided by behavior analysis. We might decide that we can predict the individual's prayer behavior by reference to our having observed this behavior reinforced by zucchini. We might further understand and demonstrate that we can modify that behavior by changing the very reward sequence we have observed.

On the other hand, although a similar analysis of the individual's flag-saluting behavior might lead us to conclude that the individual salutes the flag because he or she is reinforced each day by a smile from the teacher, this analysis does not allow us to explain or predict "flag-saluting behavior" in the society at large as well as would an analysis of the political history and customs of the group. This history is both a record of past behaviors and of beliefs that people hold with respect to those behaviors. The beliefs they hold quite often, but not always, reveal an internal logic to those believers whether or not the beliefs match the ontological considerations and beliefs of the observing scientist. In part, as we have seen, social psychology has been a study of belief systems regarding other people regardless of whether or not they are true in that they match the beliefs of the observing scientist. Further, if people act (behave) consistently with a belief system, the system is, at least at one level, ipso facto true.

CHAPTER 6

Hermeneutics and Rhetoric: The Rise of the Active Organism

The past 20 years have seen an increasing emphasis on the idea that an organism actively contributes to the processes that psychologically characterize it. The passivity of the organism, assumed in the older forms of behaviorism, is apparently an idea no longer held by the majority of social and other psychologists. Markus and Zajonc (1985), in their chapter on the cognitive perspective in the *Handbook of Social Psychology* conclude that "one can no longer view today's social psychology as the study of social behavior. It is more accurate to define it as the study of the social mind" (p. 137). Such a conclusion represents, at least on the surface, a radical departure from the assumptions and working principals of older systems and the system of the behavior analysts discussed in the previous chapter. This contention suggests a shift toward a Kantian inspired epistemology and away from that of the British empiricists. As Johnson (1989) recently suggested, "the very term 'cognitive science' would have been deemed an oxymoron by empiricist psychologists during the 19th and early 20th centuries" (p. 27). However, the issue is complicated and we need to examine it in some detail.

Cognition

There has been an enormous amount of research on cognition during the past 20 years. Every perspective from behaviorism to phenomenology is represented in attempts to explain how human beings think. Social cognition, thought, or representation that addresses itself to some aspects of other human beings as opposed to physical objects or abstract ideas, has received similar theoretical treatment.

As one might expect, the same epistemological dichotomy between cognition as an effect produced by causal aspects of the individual or environment, and cognition as a process that can only be described as it is a product of the indigenous characteristics of the organism, is present in theories designed to explain social thought. In Markus and Zajonc's excellent review of the cognitive perspective, theories of various forms of social cognition are categorized along dimensions that either emphasize stimulus control over verbal behavior or emphasize nonreducible states of the organism that function independently of specific externally observable factors. The explanatory emphasis on cognitive structures took the form of introducing organizing principles (listed by Markus & Zajonc, 1985) such as inferential sets (Jones & Thibault, 1958), hypotheses (Bruner, 1951), theories (Epstein, 1973), scripts (Abelson, 1976), themes (Lingle & Ostrom, 1981), frames (Minsky, 1975), categories (Rosch, 1973; Smith & Medin, 1981), prototypes (Cantor, 1979; Cantor & Mischel, 1977), attitudes (Tesser & Cowan, 1975, 1977), and schemas (Neisser, 1976; Stotland & Cannon, 1972). All of these concepts are attempts to describe a structural aspect of thought and problem solving. They are invoked because the various theorists using them have not been satisfied with the idea of a passive organism determined in its behavior by causative factors beginning outside of it.

Similarity among these structural concepts and the older concepts of *einstellung,* set, and attitude are apparent. All of them are designed to offer a description of the fact that human beings do not react uniquely to each different stimulus pattern that they may encounter day by day, but rather have similar reactions based on only certain perceived aspects of a situation. This is especially true when the stimulus configuration is social or is a symbol for a social group, individual, or event. That is, we reserve individual, idiosyncratic responses for people we know well or are interested in knowing well. Contrary to this, any individual with, for example, an appropriate blue uniform, is reacted to in the same manner as any other when we need a policeman. As discussed in chapter 1, the appearance of a blue uniform activates a set of beliefs, opinions, and behaviors regarding the individual who wears it. This kind of "set," "attitude," "schema," etc., is the result of a virtual biological process needed for survival because an organism cannot take the time to specifically evaluate the individual characteristics of every person he or she encounters in daily life. Animals generalize in a similar manner for the same biological reasons. Most cognitive theories hold that cognitive structures are learned over time, but the implication is that learning always produces a readiness to respond to social stimuli in a certain way that will then influence other learning experiences. The further implication is that a theory analyzing behavior alone is not adequate, by itself, to explain social reactions. In short, the individual contributes to social perception as well as does the stimulus conditions that he or she reacts to and interprets.

Various cognitive theories that have developed to explain social mind assume that human beings are both active and creative in their social perceptions and their consequences, which yields behavior, in part unaffected by behavioral contingencies. The active structures take the various forms already listed, as, inferential sets, schemas, categories, etc. These various nonbehavioral models require descriptive, interpretive, that is, hermeneutical analysis, both of individual cognitive structures and of the social structures that develop as a consequence. The argument that given the existence of cognitive structures in an active organism, certain characteristics of social structures will follow, is ancient and is made specifically by such theorists as Giambattistta Vico (1961), Karl Jung (1956), and others. Society is seen as a product of the contingencies of environment heremeneutically assessed by individuals utilizing certain active characteristics of thought. Hermeneutics is both the method by which one comes to know the structure of society and a characteristic of the structure of social mind.

HERMENEUTICS AND THE DIALECTIC

A fascinating and important facet of human cognition is the ability to reason both demonstratively and dialectically. The difference in the reasoning forms sets some of the dimensions of thought that illuminate the structure of society.

Mortimer Adler (1927) made three major distinctions in the way one could utilize the dialectic. Dialectic can be part of an argument designed to discover the first principles of existence (metaphysics). Dialectic as a manner of defining and analyzing a variety of problems can be placed for consideration in the realm of logic and is usually juxtaposed with demonstrative reasoning. Dialectic as a description of certain aspects of human experience apparent from reasoning can exist in the realm of explanation of human behaviors other than reasoning.

The use to which the psychologist can put the dialectic disallows any precise separation between the empirical and logical meanings of the process, because dialectic as logic necessarily implies interpretations of some human activity, besides reasoning, as dialectic in nature. The standard conception of dialectic logic is that meaning and truth are discovered by considering an idea with its opposite in order to develop a synthesis that represents a level of truth or meaning superior to the thesis and antithesis preceding it. Presumably the opposition of ideas reveals insights into an issue not before apparent. Dialectic logic is often considered as an alternative to demonstrative logic, which is reasoning from known truths and then extracting or deducing propositions already contained in the known truths. The hypothetico-deductive method as the process of making inference in science is, of course, an instance of demonstrative reasoning.

With demonstrative reasoning, the assumption is made that premises have an empirical solidity and are, therefore, indeed, "known truths," otherwise logic alone will not produce useful conclusions. The identification of reasonable premises, especially with regard to human activity, is often established by either a formal or informal dialectic reasoning on the part of the scientist or citizen who wishes to understand some aspect of human life. The ability to quickly posit the opposite condition of the one in question is both a characteristic of the dialectic and of human cognition. Thus "good" is a concept that quickly produces the idea of "bad." The requirement that both "good" and "bad" be considered alternately if one is to comprehend either one of them within the structure of society eventually leads to a moral position of some kind, if only one that rejects the dichotomy altogether as, for example, does Nietzsche (1966) in *Beyond Good and Evil.* God implies not God and, therefore atheism is an alternative to religion.

The dichotomies discussed in earlier chapters such as that between mind and body, environmental and organismic determiners of behavior, internal and external environments, and so forth, are natural dialectic qualities that are characteristic of human cognition and must be described as such. It is unlikely that they will be predictively explained by reference to environmental variables. Interestingly, dichotomous thinking is, in modern times, almost always eschewed by theorists. We are cautioned against its dangers. However, this form of reasoning is pervasive. The thesis and antithesis seem necessary to synthetically construct explanations at virtually every level of discourse. Cognitive structures are set against reinforced behavior except that one thesis is chosen over the other rather than an attempt being made to work out the dialectic consequence appearing in a synthesis of opposites.

Knowing about knowing requires the idea that the dialectic is not determined by any particular associations from the environment (Slife, 1987). Knowing that one knows requires that one consider that he or she may come to know by considering alternatives to what one believes one knows. Particular associations from the environment determine behavior that can be explained by demonstrative reasoning. Focusing upon a part of the environment to be explained entails a dialectical process that is part of the epistemological repertoire of the human organism that thus can only be described, not demonstratively analyzed. Such a synthesis, as I have suggested earlier, is possible for psychology in a number of ways such as that proposed regarding social history as a description of societal structure representing what a be-havior analyst might call the behavioral repertoire of a group of individuals living together.

Description and Interpretation

Hermeneutics has come to mean (Ricoeur, 1981) the theory of the operations of understanding in their relations to the interpretations of texts. These texts were originally the classical ones of Greco-Latin antiquity and of the Old and New Testaments. Eventually, hermeneu-tics addressed itself to any texts of literature, and finally it became a general enterprise that raised exegesis and philology to the level of a technology or method with presumed general power. When the exe-getical and philological sciences are included within historical disqui-sition, hermeneutics becomes a global enterprise for the revelation of the meaning of the history of humanity. The expansion of the nature of the text to be interpreted occurred in the late 19th century with the work of Dilthey (1977) and others. Reality itself in historical time as the goal of hermeneutics was opposed to the systematic examination impled by natural scientific laws.

Two aspects of hermeneutical analysis are possible: (a) the grammat-ical interpretation of a text or a phase of history is based on discourse that is common to a culture or an individual, or (b) interpretation is addressed to the singularity of the individual (i.e., the writer, if text is involved). The scientific enterprise, therefore, involving as it does a special, noncommon language, is not and cannot be hermeneutical. To consider the common historical and linguistic aspects of text or social milieu is to forget the individual writer or participant, and to under-stand the individual is to forget his or her language and social history. In social psychology a similar question was put by Gordon Allport as to how it is possible for the individual to create culture as he or she must, and to be part of it and, therefore, to be determined by it. This is social psychology as objective, nomothetic certum, on the one hand, and idiographic, subjective verum, on the other.

People offer signs of their own existence. To understand these signs is to understand human social activity. The signs are linguistic and gestural and occur within a sociohistorical context. These signs, in turn, yield forms in stable configurations such as evaluations, feelings, and decisions that can be deciphered by others. The deciphering in its formal aspects takes the form of philological and psychological analyses. We can understand vanished worlds such as the Roman or scholastic because each society creates its own medium of understanding by creating social and cultural worlds in which it understands itself. This universal history is the field of hermeneutics in its most modern usage. Meaning units rise above the historical flux in order for life to grasp and understand itself. For example, all civilizations at all times in the history of human beings have grappled with the idea of an omnipotent, interested (in human affairs) God, if only to reject the idea, as it is in Marxian socialism. The fact that every society has taken an explicit position with regard to the idea of God represents a characteristic or meaning that is universal among human beings. This universal way of describing themselves in terms of God has itself been examined in higher level explanatory units by many others including Freud and Jung. In all cases, the analyses are hermeneutic and not meaningfully subjected to causal analyses although causal concepts such as reinforced behavior, for example, are relevant to the total process of such social universals. Causal analyses, however, do not penetrate social history as the content of values rather than their manner of acquisition are relevant to a full comprehension of the socius.

The experiential control of variables yields information about reality that suggests the ability to control it everywhere and at any time under specifiable conditions. Life experience, for either an individual or a group of individuals living together, generates specific histories of lived events that in turn influence the course each will take in the future. Experimental science extracts from individual or group experience that which can be reconciled to a theoretical language and therefore a set of principles of control that eliminates that part of the experience that is unique.

Interpretations developed from hermeneutic analysis reverse the process of science by attempting to grasp the intentional quality of individual or group life experiences. These intentions need to be expressed in the language of the actors themselves rather than in a specialized language of the abstract. The description of concrete lived reality does not meet the requirements for being expressed in the logic of general statements (Habermas, 1971). However, general statements also are not capable of describing concrete life experience. The hermeneutic interpreter is required to adapt the language of the life experience. Ordinary language is structured so that an individual can be understood through general categories when in a dialogue. Hermeneutics can thus be said to be a methodical approach to the everyday understanding of oneself and others in the communicative experience.

There are three classes of life expressions: linguistic expressions, experiential expressions, and expressions and actions. Linguistic expressions range from those in an absolute form such as the expression of a logical statement, to those of the psychotic, which may not be understood by any other person. The meaning of a scientific statement is the same in every context in which it is used and hence is communicated completely to every individual who knows the vocabulary. Understanding of scientific statements is more complete than in any other life expression. The more linguistic expressions are linked to a concrete life context, the more important they are to a specific communicative context. Complete understanding of such life-linked statements is problematic because there will no longer be complete agreement as to meaning. If linguistic expressions are totally alien, hermeneutic interpretation is impossible. On the other hand, hermeneutics are unnecessary if there is nothing alien in linguistic expressions. The goal of science and logic is to make statements about reality that require no interpretation at all since the meaning is immediately and abundantly clear to all with the vocabulary.

It is the further assumption of hermeneutics that it is not possible for science and logic to achieve their goals of eliminating the necessity for hermeneutics because of the belief that dialogic use of language always requires hermeneutic interpretation. Thus social institutions, customs, attitudes (i.e., any phenomenon that is communicative and therefore social) will always be in need of hermeneutic interpretation even though some parts of the social process may be amenable to understanding by the pure language of logic and science. Suppose I am standing with an individual who has been diagnosed psychotic and, as he looks out of the window he says, "It is a dog-bite day." I reply, thinking that he is referring to the weather, "How can you say that, the sun is shining brilliantly, it is warm, the flowers are in bloom, and the birds are singing." He says, "Nevertheless, it is a dog-bite day." With no other information, no one would be able to interpret his statement. Interpretation within the dialogue is almost impossible. However, had the man's mother received the same communication she would immediately have been able to interpret his remark to *mean* that this was just the kind of day on which he was bitten badly by a vicious dog when he was 6 years old. Her interpretation is possible because she possesses information about the unique life circumstances of her son that allows her to interpret, correctly, his seemingly incoherent statement. Presumably, a clinical psychologist might eventually learn to correctly interpret various dialogue with the patient after having learned some of his unique life context. In a less extreme situation, one can witness the ability of a mother to understand and interpret the odd word and sound usages not infrequently made between twins in dialogue with one another, although they are incomprehensible to an outsider.

Considering what most of us think of as ordinary dialogue among people in the same social group, interpretation is clearly still both necessary and cannot be substituted for by a scientific analysis. As we have seen, the analysis of verbal behavior is directed more toward constructing a system that accounts for the acquisition of vocabulary and speech forms more than it accounts for the unique use to which different people and different verbal groups put language.

Meaning is also given not only by language, but by intentional action as well. Intentional action is subject to norms active within the context in which the actor places herself. Actions need interpretation as to this intentional meaning. In short, people cannot always, and do not expect to, be taken at their word. People expect their actions, particularly the intentional ones, to be interpreted. Psychologists appreciate hermeneutic analysis within the framework of Freudian diagnosis and psychoanalysis where interpretation of nonverbal actions are crucial to the success of therapy. Psychoanalysis also clearly illustrates the hermeneutic necessity of the interpreter being both familiar with, and part of, the process being interpreted and yet remaining distant from it.

Experiential expression refers to the nonverbal, unintentional expressions such as gestural, physiognomic, or mimic responses. Blushing, growing pale, nervous glances, fighting, laughing, crying, and so on, need to be interpreted as well. Experiential expression is taken as a signal of unstatable intentions and of those unstable reactions (both known and unknown by the subject) that are nonetheless individual and socially meaningful.

Ordinary language is the means by which people correctly or incorrectly interpret these hermeneutic components. The skilled interpreter creates a system that yields a coherent interpretation of life context. Freud is clearly the most famous and perhaps most skilled in hermeneutic analysis even though he envisages his system to be scientifically established, biologically based theory in the positivism tradition. Habermas (1971) concluded that psychoanalysis is the "only tangible example of a science incorporating methodical self-reflection" (p. 214). I believe Habermas is correct. It is this combining of self-reflection with biology that has made Freud's system impossible to classify and alien to most positivistic psychological theories, Dollard and Miller's attempt at reconciliation notwithstanding.

What is behind active memory is what is to be accounted for in Freudian analysis. The way to interpret the unconscious is to consider the symbols that are given in linguistic and experiential expressions and those in intentional actions. Unintended expressions need to be interpreted so that psychoanalysis links hermeneutics with causal analysis. It is this fact that has puzzled psychologists for years about the nature of psychoanalytic theory and therapy. When attempts have been made to cast all of psychoanalysis into the terms of causal analysis (e.g., Dollard & Miller, 1950), they have fallen short because they have not accounted for the hermeneutic quality of the system. When psychoanalysis is viewed as an artistic endeavor to aid people, the essential biological progression of the psychosexual stages is lost to interpretation.

A similar condition exists analogously within the framework of social psychological theory. Causal analyses exclude the hermeneutic possibilities of historical and institutional interpretation, whereas the latter do not consider causal lines that are helpful in describing certain objective attributes of the social context. For example, in attribution research, it has been argued (e.g., Kelley, 1973; Wortman, 1976) that people make causal attributions in an attempt to maintain a feeling of control in the world. If an accident is attributed to specific situational or dispositional factors of the victim, it is less likely that we will perceive ourselves as future "candidates." If the accident is attributed to chance, then there is nothing we can do to prevent ourselves from being the victim in another "uncontrollable" situation; that is, we cannot avoid our own victimization. This theory is closely related to Lerner's (1975) and Walster's (1966) "just world hypothesis." That is, individuals believe in a just world where people get what they deserve and deserve what they get. Walster has found that a person's desire to avoid victimization influences not only the causal attributions he or she makes, but the tendency to punish those who cause accidents. Thus if the results of an accident—or of any event for that matter—are positive, either the recipients are seen as meritorious, or the event is attributed to chance, thus allowing the attributor to believe that he or she might be a candidate for a similar positive accident in the future. If, however, the results are negative, then not only the recipient's characteristics are degraded, but the outcome is attributed to specific situational or dispositional factors to make certain that we exclude ourselves from being the recipients of such outcomes in the future. In life, outcomes can rarely be clearly attributable to chance or to being caused by identifiable factors even when the situation is analyzed by use of logic and science. No one, trained or not, can easily separate the various events associated with an accident into either chance or causal categories. If someone crosses a street against the traffic signal and is struck by an automobile, a causative explanation of the event is possible, but chance can play a role because people who cross against the traffic signal are not invariably or even frequently struck by automobiles. Regardless of whether people make causal or chance attributions on a logically and evidentiary secure basis, the fact that they make them at all, and in certain patterns, is of great social significance. A crucial problem for the attribution researcher is how attributions develop and change over time and circumstance within various group histories and how this development characterizes the decisionary process in the social situation.

Intentional action and experiential and linguistic expressions exist in dialectical arrangements with one another and what one makes out of life; that which one derives from one's experience is the product of the fusion of the dialectical oppositions of life (e.g., absurdity vs. meaning, causality vs. chance). An event or outcome is often both negative and positive, involving both causality and chance (e.g., winning at poker); discovering the event's significance for the individual requires that one go beyond a causal analysis and come to understand the particular meaning it has for the individual. In order to do this, an interpretation of the individual's context is necessary. Attribution researchers (Jones & Nisbitt, 1971) have found that actors attribute their actions to situational factors whereas observers attribute the same actions to the personal dispositions of the actor. In such experiments, observers are usually instructed to pay attention to the actor whereas the latter is unaware of the observers.

Buss (1978) has argued that actors attribute their actions to situational requirements because they are attempting to justify and explain these actions. Observers attribute the same actions to dispositions because they are "outside" of the action and can attribute causal influences that are presumably operating on the actor. The two explanations are not of the same logical type (see Buss, 1978, for details). Error in the observer's analysis is more easily checked than in the actor's. The observer's causal analysis of the actor's behavior, because it is causal, is subject to an empirical demonstration of truth or falsity no matter how difficult such an experiment might be to construct. On the contrary, the actor's reasons for his or her actions are not subject to causal analysis. These reasons might require little interpretation if the actor is astute and trained in logic and science. Then again, interpretation might have to be made in the terms of ordinary language with attention to linguistic and experiential expressions and intentional action. Generally, situational-dispositional dichotomies with emphasis on one or the other pole, reflect the interpretative distinction that theorists from before Descartes to the present seem never to be able to eliminate.

One suggestion that arises from this impasse is of course, that various theorists are referring to different levels (Doise, 1986) of the same, continuing problem. Once the possibility arises that theories of social psychology are addressing *different* aspects of the problem of explaining human action, some of the dichotomies give way. The idea that there are various levels of analysis that are appropriate to the total enterprise of explaining the social is inherent in the conceptual separation of social psychology from sociology. Although there are clearly techniques and subject matter that overlap in the efforts of practitioners of both areas, there remains the idea that each is focused upon different aspects of what is social and what is not.

Social psychologists do not stray very far from considering individual reactions to various social stimuli. The concepts of attitude, attribution, set, belief, and so forth, are both applied to, and measured in, single individuals and then, usually by application of statistical analyses, referred to groups. Although sociologists are interested in the same problems, many deal with conceptualized aspects of society such as institutions that have characteristics and structures that can be described without reference to individuals. Contrast the ideas of "attitude" on the one hand and "marriage" on the other. A consideration of attitude, as we have seen, requires attention to psychological processes involved in individual reactions such as the ability to generalize stimuli and react similarly to them. Marriage as an institution, on the other hand, forces us to take a historical stand in order to develop either a comparative analysis among many cultures or a developmental one extending over the history of the group. These various levels develop because of the focus of the social psychologist on various aspects of the activity of people in social situations. Hence the idea of levels is fundamentally epistemological and does not refer to the subject's perception of his or her activity.

As an illustration of how different theorists might approach the same behavior at different levels of analysis, we may consider the situation that was introduced earlier in contrasting behavior analysis with more molar forms of explanation. We may accept the contention that a child both behaves and can talk and think about that behavior. When a child learns to tie her shoe, we may accept the explanation that various correct movements with the shoelace were reinforced by her mother smiling, patting, and saying, "Very good." We may also accept the explanation that the child's use of words such as, "I can tie my shoes," or, "I make a bow with the shoelace," were reinforced in a similar manner by the mother. In addition, we can accept an analysis of the shared meaning of such words when the same individual, years later, discusses methods of fastening shoes that have developed over the centuries. That is, our explanation no longer focuses on the acquisition of words, but on the context of meaning of the words that no longer requires the invocation of reinforcement as a principal of explanation. Individuals can share information and beliefs and discuss them in detail meaningfully, without reference as to how the words used were acquired in the first place. The level of inquiry has shifted from analysis of acquisition of behavior to analysis of structure and form of behavior as it is used after acquisition.

This latter level of analysis requires concepts in addition to those of reinforcement because the individual has a behavioral repertoire that is, in part, genetically determined. A description of those given characteristics might take the form of Chomsky's analysis of the deep structure of language, for example. On this argument, the behavioral analysis and the context description of the same phenomena are not necessarily incompatible, but rather are focused on different levels of its appearance.

RHETORIC

Explanations at different levels are, of course, constructed to convince both the theorist and others of the legitimacy of the explanation by empirical demonstration and logical argument. The introduction of rhetoric into the affairs of social psychology is a refocusing of both level and kind of analysis applied to certain aspects of the problem of explaining social activity.

Rhetoric is an attempt to reach the truth through public discourse; that is, through the hermeneutic discourse of an interpreter of the nature of society. One individual tries to convince another by fitting words to carefully chosen facts. This implies that there are other facts not chosen by a particular rhetorician, thus an interpretation of society or an aspect of it is in competition with other interpretations. This, however, is not unlike multiple interpretations of the same phenomenon that occur in traditional science before a single theory is chosen as correct. Even then, we have often seen the submergence of such "correct" theories into other, more inclusive theories at a later date. By a convincing argument that may be logically and empirically sound and emotionally appealing, one convinces another of his or her view of that social world. If the listener is convinced, both share a similar view of that world and behave accordingly. Considering that there are many possible views of the world, the interesting issue is whether or not generalities can be formed from the overlap among them. The overlap in interpretations of social life may be subjected to experiment to gain a certain kind of information, as in the attributions studies showing similar causal interpretations given by people observing similar social situations. On the other hand, as the different views of the same social context may be more significant in their diversity than in their commonality, we are thrown back on hermeneutics and rhetoric to describe the phenomena.

Vico believed that because our experience was far richer than our language, we modify the way we speak to enrich language in an attempt to match our experience (Mooney, 1985). Consequently he concluded that certain linguistic forms (e.g., metaphors) are not abuses of language, but rather are an attempt to match experience verbally. Every language lacks words to match experience. Therefore, people create tropes, words with transferred meanings (i.e., words used in a sense other than the one that is primary to them), in order to communicate the richness of experience. These transferred meanings are created in four predictable ways: By metaphor, from one thing to something similar (my love is a red, red rose); by metonymy, from cause to effect or effect to cause (Have you read Tolstoy?); syneckdoche, from the whole to the part or visa versa ("All hands on board," or "Enter France [Shakespeare]); irony, from one thing to its opposite (beautiful job! [meaning bad job]). These tropes are not mere figures of speech used by the rhetorician in order to convince, they are part of the way thought works through speech and are universal.

Rhetoric, within the context of a modern state, is the means by which social images and ideas are formed and by which a people define themselves. In America, one such image is that of the self-sufficient, frontier cowboy myth that is believed and is emulated by many people. The *elan vital* of Bergson and the French is a similar communicated rhetorical production that actually shaped behavior.

Billig (1987) has argued that classical persuasion studies during World War II of the kind begun by Hovland and his associates, is a form of rhetorical research in that the fundamental question asked is: Under what circumstances of communication do people adjust their perception of the social world to coincide with that of the communicator? Put this way, this is indeed a rhetorical question. Billig likens the goal of this research to that of Plato's plan for a science of rhetoric in the Phaedrus.

In the 1969 edition of this book, I observed the following:

> While working in the area of persuasive communication for a number of years, I became increasingly aware of what I thought to be a curious fact about research in this area including my own work. We were almost always concerned with aspects of the communication situation which had little to do with the content, that is, with the empirical and logical aspects of the

message that was being communicated. Most of us were interested in one or more of the following variables: the controversality of the issue referred to in the communication, the awareness by the subject of the manipulatory intent of the communicator, the style used by the communicator, his prestige, the length of the communication, the medium (television, radio) used to transmit the communication, and other variables of this type as well. . . . This research focus was not an accident of the interest patterns of the various psychologists doing work in communication. Of that I was convinced. Was it a natural by-product of American behaviorist tradition to focus on just about anything but meaning, or was something more fundamental operating? . . . Psychologists were focusing on such things as the kind of medium used to convey the message, the style of the speaker, etc., because these very characteristics were messages in themselves. Prestige conveys information. A tape recorder conveys different information than does television, even though the empirical referents of the words and the logical structure of their arrangement are the same in both cases. . . . These all yield information different from the information conveyed by the ideas in the content of the message. This content, is in itself, another message providing other information. (pp. 162–163)

The reader will recognize Marshall McLuhan's influence in the contention that medium is also message. This notwithstanding, a broader interpretation of this observation made 20 years ago is that there is and has always been a rhetorical quality to any communication, particularly those designed to persuade regarding social content. It may be odd to conceive of a physical object such as a television receiver to be a rhetorical device, but if such an object conveys a characteristically different message from another activity, such as a radio, then at least an analogy with the devices of rhetoric can be maintained. In both cases, what is true and is believed is a function of the ability of the rhetorician to convince, because there are no absolute answers to be discovered.

People's interpretation of the structure and function of their society will obviously be diverse. We know that there is a spoken, publicly agreed upon set of values and rules under which a group purports to function, but there are also other interpretations by the same people as to how their group actually functions. For example, we often hear it said about America that it values loyalty to country and respect for its symbols such as the national flag, the office of the president, and so on, and that it is governed by the will of its people expressed in their freely voting for candidates for political office. It is also common for some citizens to hold the opinion that the country is really governed by industrial and military special interest groups for their own gain and that the average citizen is powerless. An individual may, indeed, believe both interpretations at the same time, viewing American public patriotism as truly felt, but being tempered by political economic reality.

There is an implied dialectic in this sort of opposed interpretations that social reality produces whatever are the extant, functioning reactions and beliefs of a citizenry. People, of course, may also construct their own views of physical reality, but in that instance traditional science convinces most people of one physical nature rather than another. Because people construct social reality in a way that they do not construct physical reality, the technique used to explain this social reality is hermeneutic and rhetorical rather than scientific and experimental. This is not to say that scientific analysis based upon experiment is not useful in delineating some of the objectively determinable conditions of social existence, such as the process of the acquisition of behaviors enlisted in social activity, but this analysis remains complementary to hermeneutic description.

In summary, there are levels of order in the social world that can be arranged as follows:

1. Order within the individual personality, the means of learning, perceiving, behaving generally. A social moment is exclusively part of the biological and behavioral characteristics of the human organism and is, therefore, predictable and potentially explainable by experimental analysis that excludes the historical aspect in the short term.

2. Order within the functioning group. People set rules and customs for themselves in order to live together based on their past experience.

3. Order within the group over historical time. Occurrences and ideas to which the group adheres or which are invoked when decisions are made.

   (a) A pattern of orderly progression of social changes that allows for prediction, but without cyclical changes.

   (b) A pattern of orderly progression of social changes that allows for prediction by the description of cycles observed over long historical periods.

4. A social moment is unexpected and unrepeatable and can only be recorded and added to other unrelated, unrepeatable social moments such as wars, elections, etc.

5. Disorder–chaos–social reality follows no discernible pattern.

As we have seen in chapter 1, there are cycles in the kind of explanations that are favored by social psychologists that change from generation to generation. These epistemological shifts quite often represent swings between the poles of some form of nativism and some form of belief in humans as tabula rasa. These epistemological cycles occur because the science of social process does not exist outside of the process itself. Social psychology and social theory in general are moments in the process of society unlike, for example, the science of physics that is not such a moment except in a trivial way, of the process involving objects in space. The methods and concepts of social science are only abstract for convenience, not, as in physics, by necessity.

As we have seen, observation of human social context can be characterized by an alienating distance of the observer from that which is observed. The observer has, therefore, altered or eliminated his or her relationship to the group and to the historical per se. There results a paradox of alienation, a tension between proximity and distance that is essential to historical consciousness. An examination of cycles in human social affairs is, of course, the job of hermeneutics. It convinces us or not depending upon the skill of the rhetoric used by the interpreter. As we have seen previously, although a rational enterprise, hermeneutics does not utilize experiment and the scientific method to come to its conclusions. Rather, hermeneutical social description needs to be added to the list of techniques utilized by the social psychologist in describing and explaining human sociality.

The forms of social explanation already listed give us a picture of the current and potential avenues of social psychological inquiry. Gergen (1973) has dealt with the fourth form, but it leaves little for the social psychologist to do, so it tends to be rejected by most theorists. The history of modern American social psychology encompasses Forms 1 and 3a. Form 5 removes us from the field of inquiry and for that reason alone is unacceptable. It is the cyclical explanation (Form 3b) that provides us with a new, fifth possibility by reinforcing the old idea that social process, although constantly changing, returns to similar patterns again and again. Forms 2 and 3 as listed, along with the idea of social history and explanation about that history occurring in cycles, allow for order and universality in explaining human beings living together. These forms assume that social behavior is both orderly and that the patterns of order are discoverable. The application of the techniques and concepts of experimental science to social data is the core of Forms 2 and 3. The concept of cycles in the history of social affairs yields another possibility for discerning order in social existence.

CHAPTER 7

Social Images in Theories of Psychology

It is clear that there are competing theories in social psychology to explain the same phenomena. To this point, I have examined the differences in assumptions and forms of these major attempts at dealing with social activity. As these systems change and compete through the years, it is rare that one convincingly demonstrates the inadequacy of the other. Kuhn (1970), of course, has dealt with this observation in his concept of paradigms of scientific thinking, but his argument has been geared principally to the natural sciences. The human sciences, particularly social psychology, as we have seen, present different problems in addition to those shared with the natural sciences.

The conflict among apparently competing theories in social psychology in particular, and psychology as a whole, can be described in a number of ways:

Of two systems purporting to predict and explain the same phenomena,

1. Either one system of explanation is true and the other is false, or both are false;

   or

2. One system is reducible to the other system;

   or

3. One system is addressing different issues than the other system.

I can think of no instance in the history of psychology where one theoretical system has convincingly demonstrated to all involved that it is correct and that another is incorrect in predicting and explaining the same phenomenon. Possibly Kohler's admission that the behavior-ists were correct and his "insight" hypothesis wrong regarding learning in chimpanzees might be one such instance. In his 1959 *American Psychologist* article, Kohler declared that, insight ". . . refers to the fact that, when we are aware of a relation, this relation is not experienced as a fact by itself, but rather as something that follows from the characteristics of the objects under consideration" (p. 729). When primates attempt to solve a problem, their behavior often shows that they are aware of a certain important relation, but when they make use of this "insight," and this solves their problem, the result can be called "solution by insight." Becoming aware of a certain relation that solves a problem can occur for many reasons, one of which is the amount of previous reinforcement with objects in the relationship as Kohler suggests indirectly. In short, The Hullian school's experimental demonstrations that previous reinforcement with sticks and boxes allows a primate to solve a problem more quickly than without that previous experience is more parsimonious an explanation of "insight" learning than Kohler's description made prior to 1959. However, Kohler did not thereby reject the general gestalt hypothesis in favor of those of behavioral theory.

Psychological theories have never been so complete nor detailed so as to successfully, even on an informal basis, reduce the terms of one to another. Dollard and Miller's attempt to recast certain Freudian prin-ciples into those of Hull's system was such an attempt, but its success is highly problematic. John Dollard and Neal E. Miller in their 1950 book, *Personality and Psychotherapy,* believed that the insightful work of Freud and Pavlov could be combined through the terms of Hull's behavior theory to build a scientifically sound explanation of the nature of personality and neurosis. By so doing, a psychotherapy consistent with this orientation could also be developed. Dollard and Miller's effort is very interesting from a number of points of view, but in this context it is especially useful as an example of a system that predated the behavior analyst's attempts to translate the terms and conceptions of other theories into their own. The authors give full credit to Freud for his insight into the nature of personality, but believe his system suffered from the lack of ability to empirically specify all of its terms. Dollard and Miller attempted to remedy the situation.

The stated goal of their effort was to write a book on psychotherapy, ". . . formulating in behavior theory and culture concepts what is done by the therapist and patient" (p. vii). Because "behavior theory" and "culture concepts" are kept separate, and presumably equal, in the statement of their goal, Dollard and Miller tacitly accept that there may be processes involved in cultural development that are not amenable to behavior theory (of the Hullian variety), at least for the time frame in which they worked. They saw themselves bringing together the traditions of Freud, Pavlov, Hull, Thorndike, and social science (social psychology, sociology). Further social science was said to *describe* (italics mine) conditions under which human beings learn. This position is not unlike that of this book.

Dollard and Miller accepted Freud's ideas that mental life was lawful and that the unconscious was significant in determining behavior. Freud's hypotheses were considered to be a rich source of significant research problems that needed to be addressed in order to develop behavioral laws. They saw Freud's hypotheses as lacking vigorous control, which they would provide by operationally recasting them into the behavioral terms of Clark Hull.

Dollard and Miller assumed that the development of neurosis and the therapy to deal with it followed the laws of learning. It was therefore necessary to translate or reconceive certain Freudian concepts into behavioral terms that would preserve the insights of Freud while allowing for the constriction of operational definitions of key terms that would allow propositions to be tested by experiment.

The "principle of reinforcement" is substituted for Freud's "pleasure principle." Ego strength is translated into an account of the higher mental processes and a description of culturally valuable learned drives and skills. Repression is redefined as the inhibition of cue-producing responses that mediate thinking and reasoning. Transference is seen as a special case of the wider concept of generalization. The dynamics of conflict behavior are systematically deduced from general learning theory. Repression and suppression are replaced by the parallel concepts of inhibition and restraint. Drive-reduction, consistent with Hull's fourth postulate, is an important therapeutic goal.

Without delving into the specifics of Dollard and Miller's translation of Freud into the behavior theory largely developed by Hull, these examples should capture the flavor of the effort. One can only wonder at Freud's reaction to it. I suspect he would have been in agreement with much of it so far as the formulation of his theories of psychosexual development and the tripartite theory of personality. However, Freud, as did others at the time of the publication of *Personality and Psychotherapy*, would have objected to psychoanalysis as a technique for prognosis and treatment being especially amenable to reduction to the terms of Hullian behavior theory.

Freud's therapy required such a long time for success because the process involved the restructuring of various life experiences. This involved the development of "insight" by the patient into his or her unconscious motivations for particular patterns of behavior. With new experience and insight, an attempt could then be made to change the patient's behavior and perception as well as that of the significant others around him or her. It is not so much that Dollard and Miller's attempt to provide a strong empirical and inferential base to Freud's theories failed, so much as it was not relevant to many essential parts of Freud's ideas, especially those concerned with the success of therapy. In any case, Freudians largely remained Freudians, and behavior theory evolved in directions that maintained the separation of the two positions.

That leaves us with the third observation, that one system may be addressing different problems than another system and thus only appear to be contradictory to it. This point is one that I have stressed throughout the book and is one whose implications need further discussion. In order to put a particular slant on this possibility, I would like to consider an analysis made in 1967 by Maurice Friedman in his book, *To Deny Our Nothingness—Contemporary Images of Modern Man.*

IMAGES OF HUMAN EFFORT

For Friedman, the "image of man" is a moral image that is prescriptive of an exemplary way of living one's life. "Image" in this sense helps human beings, in every age, rediscover their humanity or rediscover what they can become. Friedman quotes Malraux in *The Walnut Trees of Altenberg.* "The greatest mystery is not that we have been flung at random among the profusion of the earth and the galaxy of the stars, but that in this prison we can fashion images of ourselves sufficiently powerful to deny our nothingness" (p. 17). From this inspiration, Friedman set out to review those "Images" that seemed to govern the actions of modern people. He was concerned with "potentiality, choice, and decision," which is a concern related to, but still different from, human beings as scientists, technicians, and observers.

These images of human moral possibility change from generation to generation, but often the themes are repeated and all are concerned with concrete lived life. What I propose are "images" in psychological explanation encompassing theories of the nature of human existence that, although not having been developed in order to provide authentic, that is, moral ways of life for human beings, neither are they divorced from them. I am proposing a parallel concept, an analogue to Friedman's sense of the "Image" of human existence regarding what I believe are images in a similar sense developed by psychological theorists over the years. There are strong epistemological and value implications to these psychological images.

Why "Images" and not simply different theories or systems of psychology? They are images in a similar sense to Friedman's use of the term because each position represents what humans beings *can* be like, but are not necessarily like. Theories, although differing among themselves, may share the same psychological image. For example, both neobehaviorists and behavior analysts share an image of human existence by their position that human behavior is to be explained exactly as any other animal behavior (i.e., by the same theory and conception).

Interestingly, Isidor Chein utilized the concept of the "image of man" in a 1972 book entitled *The Science of Behavior and the Image of Man*. Chein's principal thesis was that psychology utilizes two major images of human existence, viewing human beings as active, responsible agents, or as being helpless, powerless reagents in essence controlled by their biology and the external environment. These positions, Chein said, are embodied in the two major behavioral positions of neobehaviorism and existential psychoanalysis. Chein further contended that the results of study and research of these two groups can result in what he called "verity" or "truth." Truth is that which is sought by science and controlled by data. Verity cannot be controlled by data but is nonetheless self-evident as subconscious awareness, for example, which is more or less a matter of definition. Verity is thus given in what it means to experience anything. One knows and acts on believed, valid information without being able to demonstrate the validity of such propositions by the tools of science. These products of the two practitioners to reflect different images of human existence (verity and truth) are closely parallel to the distinction made by Vico (chapter 2) between verum (truth) and certum (certainty). Certum being the product of a scientific enterprise that produces probable results and verum a product of the constructed experience of the individual and the group over time (that which is made by human beings). I return to Chein's position later. Friedman's conception of image needs to be expanded and examples of his analysis given in order to set the stage for my own effort.

Friedman is clear on what he means by image—it is a possibility of what human beings can be and is always positive; that is, the image is a moral one. A single individual may share, at any one time, several of these images and they may be active in his or her life successively at different stages of change and development. Some of the images that Friedman discusses are:

1. The Modern Socialist. Abstracted from concrete, constantly changing social reality as with socialist revolutionaries or, more recently, conservative revolutionaries against the welfare state. This

position Friedman saw as embodied in the works of Andre Malraux, Arthur Koestler, Ignazio Silone, and Carlo Levi.

2. The Modern Vitalist. The position that values dynamic, creative intuitive life higher than the pursuit of an abstract idea. Representatives of this position are Henri Bergson and Nikos Kazantzakis.

3. The Modern Mystic. A sense of the immanence of God in a lived reality, such as one's work or family. T. S. Eliot, Martin Buber, and Aldous Huxley's work are taken as examples of this position.

4. The Modern "Saint." Serving God by becoming more human in concrete lived life. Carlo Coccioli, George Bernanos, and Graham Greene's novels reflect this position.

5. Psychological Man. Friedman concedes that Freud's vision of human beings is an image of man as are the others, but Freud accomplishes this by substituting the process of superego as it functions with those of id and ego for the earlier notion of conscience or moral sense based on the free decisions of the individual. In so doing, Freud has synthesized ". . . two antithetical traditions, mechanism and rationalism, on the one hand, and romanticism and mysticism, on the other" (p. 191). Human beings thus exist in those processes that are determined by the passions (biologically linked) and the expectations of society. Value lies in bringing the unconscious into the conscious; that is, the conscious realization of unconscious biological forces allows the individual, ideally, to deal with his or her sense of morality and develop it so that it neither destroys the individual nor society.

As suggested earlier, it is possible for an individual to move through each of these images at various stages in his or her life or to embrace parts of them at any one stage. All of the images listed are possible ways that a human being may view him or herself in the context of a concrete life. One is no more "correct" than the other. The images represent what human beings can be and how they can act with regard to others. Friedman views them as "authentic" images, in contrast to "inauthentic" images. Inauthentic images represent what is lacking in an age and are manifested in people's behavior at the time. An image that is inauthentic is one in which human values are "truncated or twisted, hypocritical or "seeming," or reflect the desire to escape from the human condition, from the necessity of taking responsibility for the values one creates in order to be in any true sense a man" (p. 28). Friedman considers the themes in Gide's *The Counterfeiters,* Malraux's *Man's Fate,* and Eliot's *The Wasteland* to be examples of inauthentic images. In short, escaping from the human conditions of suffering and loneliness accomplished through the taking of drugs, through violence, mythomania, or revolution is inauthentic. Accepting the human condition is part of the authentic images of human existence. Personal commitment through entering and communicating with others is the core of authentic existence.

I believe that Friedman's concept of "images of man" contains an insight into human possibility that is useful in reconceiving various epistemological positions in psychology. Chein's (1972) distinction between thinking of human beings as passive or active, as reagents or initiators, are two fundamentally different assumptions about the nature of human existence. These assumptions still separate psychologists and particularly social psychologists. However, it now seems possible to extend Friedman and Chein's analyses to see more clearly how diverse epistemologies in psychology may be brought closer together than had previously been the case.

Psychological epistemologies, to be enumerated later, are not necessarily moral stances or, therefore, "images" in Freidman's sense. They are, however, related to moral positions. I suggest four psychological "images" that I call *The Mechanical Image, The Behavioral Image, The Cognitive Image,* and *The Historical Image.* These "images" share many beliefs and are different with regard to others, but the core of the differences among them is the position each takes as to the source of change, movement, and modification of human behavior, including thought. Clearly these images can also be described as having different ontologies and epistemologies, but they are not necessarily characterized by differences in these areas. What makes each position an "image" rather than merely characterized by differences in epistemology, theoretical, or ontological structure, is that certain belief about the nature of human existence follows from each position that very quickly becomes enmeshed in a moral stance.

The Mechanical Image

To my knowledge, there are no current systems in psychology that are fundamentally mechanical in nature. This image is now a historical precursor of later systems. A mechanical system requires an implicit or explicit belief that behavior or action is the result of a causative chain where there are no time gaps between any cause and its effect. In the past the behavioral systems of John Watson (1913) and Clark Hull (1943, 1952) were mechanical. For example, Hull's "fractional antedating goal reaction" (used in explaining increased running speed of rats in a straightaway) is described as a series of environmental stimuli continuously linked to responses with no time gaps between, thus qualifying the process as a mechanical causal sequence. The sequence is described formally in Hull's *A Behavior System* (1952):

Corollary xv
When a stimulus (S) or a stimulus trace (s) acts at the same time that a hitherto
unrelated response (R) occurs and this coincidence is accompanied by an
antedating goal reaction (r_g), the secondary reinforcing powers of the stimulus evoked by the latter (s_g) will reinforce S to R, giving rise to a new S → R
dynamic connection. (p. 125)

In addition, Hull's Postulate 4, containing the well-known drive-
reduction proposition, is linked to afferent and efferent processes that
had, in earlier postulates, been described as continuous impulses in the
nervous system, thus assuring an epistemology dependent upon mechanical causation as an underlying assumption. In social psychology
no one has ever attempted a thoroughgoing mechanical, causative
explanation of social behavior if one excludes as possible exceptions
Ross' theory of suggestion and MacDougall's instinct theory of the
early 20th century.

The Behavioral Image

The behavioral image requires belief in the contention that environmental conditions determine the behavior of a fixed biological entity.
The behavior determined can vary with the nature of the biological
entity or with environmental conditions, or both. Although there have
been many attempts at using early behaviorist considerations in explaining social behavior, the more sophisticated position of the behavior analysts is considered under this rubric.

The Cognitive Image

Central to this position is the assumption that what is ordinarily called
thought or verbal behavior is often independent of *specific* environmental influence. That is, specific causal chains of environmental
events and biological conditions do not always determine thought or
verbal behavior. Rather, the innate characteristics of the human organism simply operate (or are genetically "programmed" in some
analyses) to react in a certain way. The job of such a cognitive theorist
is to describe the way this process works. This image is often in conflict
with the behavioral image.

The Historical Image

The historical image is, as we have seen in Vico's new science, the
position that an individual living through specific experiences with

other members of a group or groups will construct, in part, his or her own world based upon those experiences. In short, lived group experiences themselves are the context in which one fashions one's social reality. In order to comprehend that world, a historical description of group life is necessary.

Assumptive Commonalities Among Psychological Images

The modern psychological images represented by the mechanical, the behavioral, the cognitive, and the historical have certain assumptions in common. These assumptions refer to the characteristics of human existence that are believed to be true, but that are not to be addressed by the particular system of explanation in question. Of course, all explanatory systems make assumptions regarding the characteristics of their subject matter that do not enter the theory as variables. Indeed, it would be extremely difficult to find a system of explanation of human existence that did not, in some way, share the assumptions that are discussed here.

The Biological Status of Humanity.   The four psychological images all assume that human beings have certain describable, genetically given characteristics that are essential to the way they behave. Human beings cannot, no matter how hard they try, duplicate the movement of birds that we call flying without being aided by mechanical devices. Birds cannot duplicate that human behavior we call speech in any way human beings recognize except, perhaps, in a rudimentary way. These facts are assumed to be determined by the genetic code of each species in systems representing all of the "images." This code sets the possibilities and limits of response of the particular species in question.

We have seen that theories classifiable under the mechanical image develop specific hypotheses about the nature of biological reality, such as the manner in which afferent and efferent neurons operate. Among behavior analysts (behavioral image) biological conditions are viewed as determiners of the behavioral repertoires of the organism that, however, do not enter behavior analytic theory as active terms.

For some cognitive positions (e.g., Wiener, 1948) the tacit assumption is made that human brain function is parallel to that of digital, analog, or other forms of computers. It is only among theories embedded within the historical image that the assumption of biological determinacy is completely tacit.

The Assumption of the Influence of the Environment.   Only mystical systems of bygone eras might not include this assumption in their basic structure. Systems fitting all four images emphasize that occurrences in the environment of the organism play important roles in the shaping of human reactions. The question has become, rather, whether anything other than environment plays a role in shaping specific behavior.

The Empirical Assumption.   All images assume that the observation of human behavior, however defined, must be at the core of any method used in the accrual of information. Observation of human activities, in short, precedes all further analysis in all modern systems of psychological explanation.

Assumption of Cosmic Determination.   This is probably a corollary of the common assumption of biological determinism shared by all of the images, but it is also inclusive of certain ontological points. All of the images assume that human beings ultimately have no control over their fundamental destiny in relation to the cosmic conditions that have shaped the universe, produced life, and determined the evolution of the human species through occasional changes in the genetic code. Human beings are confined by their biology and the physical conditions of the universe in which they live. They also inevitably die, and cannot change that arrangement. Not all systems of explanation of the human condition, of course, necessarily make this assumption or we would not have institutionalized concepts such as those of heaven and hell. All of the images believe that human beings are a result of the same determining forces, largely unknown, that were involved with the shaping of everything in the universe. This is a tacit, ontological assumption.

Differences Among Psychological Images

The differences in basic assumptions among the four positions are, as one might expect, more focused and explicit than are the commonalities.

The Causative Assumption.   The concept of cause and effect and how it enters the structure of various explanatory positions in psychology has been discussed at some length in chapter 3. It may be useful to summarize conclusions at this point.

Mechanical causation is a tacit assumption of some neobehaviorist positions such as that of Clark Hull, but is not part of the assumptions of the behavior analysts. I concluded that the behavior analysts did indeed assume causative relationships to exist among the variables that entered into their predictive formulae, but those relationships were not mechanical in the sense used here.

Most cognitive systems emphasize the description of cognitive states and their operation. Often the description follows a model provided by a nonhuman system such as a computer. Because the emphasis of these cognitive systems is on description rather than prediction, the nature of cause and effect generally remains a tacit assumption more connected to what I have called *cosmic determination* than to the specific explanatory system.

Causality in historical systems, which are also ex post facto descriptive, is considered, if at all, as an epistemological product of the history of the group. All societies, pre-literate or advanced, believe that certain actions have certain necessary consequences and in that sense all assume the validity of the general causal principal in some part of their lives. This, however, fits the cosmic determination assumption more than the specific operating sense of causality intended here.

The Assumption of Locus of Control of Behavior. This, of course, as Chein (1972) and others have recognized, is the assumption that creates the greatest and most important differences among the systems. Theories classifiable under the mechanical and behavioral images assume explicitly that environmental conditions in conjunction with the biologically given possibilities for reaction in the organism, determine behavior. No mediational variables such as thought, ego, will, and so forth, need be invoked to make successful predictions and to thereby explain behavior. The explanation *is* the series of functional relationships among input and output variables that can be developed from careful observation. Thus the locus of control of behavior is in the environment.

Cognitive systems identify the locus of control in the possibilities for behavior that are part of the structure of the organism. In some cases, the organism is seen as a machine (not necessarily one that works mechanically) whose functions need to be described. Again, in some cases the model for description is some kind of existing machine such as the digital or analog computer. In other cognitive systems (Chomsky, 1964, 1966) no model is assumed and thought is described carefully in terms of its capability. In each of these approaches, the assumption is explicitly made that human beings are capable of behavior uninfluenced by specific patterns of environmental conditions. "Specific" needs to be emphasized because no "image" of any kind has anything to say about how human beings react outside of *any* environmental conditions. Given an acceptance of cosmic determination, cognitive systems maintain that human beings are capable of making decisions uninfluenced by causal chains beginning in the environment.

The historical image places locus of control for human affairs in the peculiar relationship between an individual and his or her group. Social behavior is, therefore, seen as fundamentally different from other forms of behavior, as for example, learning how to drive a car, although, of course, that has its social aspects as well. This is a very different assumption than that made by the behavioral images that all behavior, whether a reaction to physical stimuli or to other people, is of the same ontological character and therefore, must be dealt with with the same epistemological assumptions and techniques.

Language. An important derivative of the different assumptions concerning the locus of control of human beings is the assumption as to the nature of language acquisition and use. We have seen that the behavioral positions considered language behavior to be acquired in a similar manner as any other response of which the organism is capable. Therefore, to the extent that it is largely but not exclusively through language that we assess thought, it is considered to be acquired by reinforcements from the environment.

As we have seen, most cognitive positions associate thinking and problem solving with indigenous characteristics of the human organism.

The historical image holds that language acquisition and development over time is a product of the development of a particular society. Within the peculiarities of a language (the French speak French and the Swedes speak Swedish) certain basic commonalities (nouns, verbs, Chomsky's deep structure) indicate that language acquisition and use is part of both the universal biological development and the common experiences of all human beings regardless of their particular social history.

Differences in Research Focus

The older mechanical systems were careful to operationally define all of their experimental variables. This operationalism led to the results of an experiment being cast in mathematical formulas that became the predictive part of an emerging theory. Often, an operational entity was used to signal the existence of an unobserved variable whose characteristics were therefore left largely undefined. However, these hypothetical constructs were recognized as essentially unoperationalized and were treated accordingly.

Although the later behavior analysts, as we have seen, still focus upon observed behavior as the substance of human and animal existence, hypothetical constructs are eliminated as viable aspects of theory building. No unobserved entities enter the functional statements built from behavioral research (see chapter 5). In both contexts, mechanical behavioral and behavior analysis, all classical problems of psychology, such as the nature of perception or of the structure of mind or of thinking, have to either be defined in terms of behavior or be relegated to the workings of the biologically given behavioral repertoire of the organism. The result is that the behavioral scientist sees the organic world as a linkage between environmental conditions and observable behavior to the exclusion of other possibilities for explanation of the same phenomena. This is at it should be, or a consistent behavioral position would not be possible.

On the other hand, cognitive theorists continually focus upon the structure of thought either as attributable to a model of some sort or a system unique in itself (as in the structural analysis of Noam Chomsky). Cognitive theorists, consequently, are always looking for order beyond behavior and environmental contingencies.

Social historians transfer their attention to evaluations and attributions people make with regard to their world and the connections with their social history. In this focus the individual or group evaluation of a phenomenon of interest to it is always valid regardless of whether or not that belief coincides with the belief of another group (such as scientists) regarding the same phenomena.

It is clear that the behavior analytic, the cognitive, and social historical images are not necessarily contradictory to one another. What they are looking at and why they are looking at it, differ.

Images-Value and Social Implications

I suggested at the beginning of this chapter that *image* was an apt term for certain differences that existed among classes of psychological theories because these classes implied different beliefs in the essence of what human life consisted. In turn, different images suggest different values, not necessarily, but as possibilities.

Let us assume that I am a confirmed behavior analyst believing in the assumptions, now all fully stated, of the system, and further believe that predictive and functional knowledge of most "psychological" aspects of human existence can be answered best by this approach. As the core of my belief system embraces the proposition that behavior is controlled by potentially knowable environmental contingencies, I must believe that my own and my friends' behavior is controlled in a similar manner. I may even plan certain reward contingencies for myself as I live my life in order to eliminate some of the gratuitous aspect of reward-behavior connections that we all experience. For example, I might say to myself, I shall reward myself with a cup of coffee after I have completed three pages of the manuscript on which I am working. This strategy may work for me better than simply working as long as I can without concern for reward after various segments of the effort. Most likely many of us have used this strategy. I may also plan such reward-behavior contingencies for my young children with some success. However, I will immediately see differences in my children's reaction to this reward system and my own. I will probably finish the manuscript whether I reward myself with coffee every so often or not. It will simply take me longer. My children, however, may not acquire the behavior of interest to me if I do not engage in some sort of reinforcement program with them. The difference is attributable to the often observed fact that adults are generally more engaged in controlling their own behavior by a variety of means than are children.

In addition, I may be concerned that a child will acquire a behavior of interest to me, solely because they are rewarded for it and will not display the behavior in similar circumstance when it is not consistently followed by similar rewards. It is understood that behavior analysts would, at this point in the discussion, introduce the ideas of response and stimulus generalization, or a shift in the nature of what is reinforcing from candy in the mouth, for example, to social approval; but that is not the point here. Without implied criticism of the behavior analytic position, it is clear that many people will hold that the "idea of reinforcement" to produce desired behavior is immoral and hence undesirable. This is not a position that is held only by a few isolated religionists, it is a position shared, in part, I suspect, by most behavior analysts. That is, *what* reinforcement increases the probability of a certain behavior is of crucial importance to most of us. We do not want to win an athletic contest because the umpire, reinforced by money from a friend, makes the calls in our favor regardless of merit. We hear parents say that they will not give their children money for receiving high grades at school because they want the reinforcement to come from the felt satisfaction of having done well, or learned something, or having been approved of by members of the society.

None of what I have said is meant to argue against the validity of the behavior analyst position. It is rather to establish that this major theory provides a certain "image" of human existence in that a moral or value-laden response, that is, concern with the nature of social reward, is bound to be a legacy of the system.

One of the most controversial issues of recent American social history concerns the means by which we reduce crime. The core issue has been, since the time of the Philadelphia Quakers, whether rehabilitation or punishment is appropriate in dealing with society's criminals. The assumption that human beings are free to make decisions because they are not necessarily determined by environmental conditions to make them necessitates a belief in the punishment of crimes. The assumption that human behavior is determined by environmental contingencies given the behavioral repertoire of the human species necessitates a belief in the rehabilitation (re-ordering of environmental conditions) in dealing with criminal behavior. In the first instance the individual is held to be the criminal and in the second the behavior is held to be criminal. Clearly two different "images" of what human beings are and can be emerge.

Certain cognitive positions (e.g., May, 1961) believe that human beings are free to make decisions. The behavioral position does not. At issue here is the difference in the core assumption concerning the locus of control of human behavior. In this example of criminal behavior, moral dilemmas arise among people who hold, more or less, to one assumption or the other. From Aristotle to Descartes to the present, there is no way to demonstrate the truth of either position, that is that human beings can or cannot make decisions uninfluenced by specific environmental contingencies. The choice of assumption is a matter of preferred *weltanschauung*. A resolution to this problem cannot take the form of empirically reasoned argument, but can proceed by emphasis on the different foci of the various images.

Differences in Focus

Leaving aside the mechanical behavioral position as of largely historical interest, it is possible to describe the noncontradictory foci of the three remaining images: the behavioral analytic, the cognitive, and the historicosocial. This description, however, does not imply that there are not still fundamental differences among the three. As we have seen, differences among the three regarding locus of control separates them in an important way.

If we wish to explain human behavior beginning with the way the brain functions as manifested in mind or thought, then the cognitive focus is appropriate. Behavior that is observable, including speech, is the focus of the behavioral image and an individual's history as they live in groups and how that history affects them is the focus of the historicosocial image. None of these foci are contradictory to one another. They are, however, different from one another, and it is difficult to imagine, given the arguments made in this book, any one of these foci, even in principal, being reduced to any of the others. Figure 7.1 summarizes differences and assumptions among the various foci of the three psychological images. Certain key elements within the three images can be compared.

Structure of Mind. From the behavioral image brain, and what other than behavior analysts would call its resulting function, mind, is taken to be the genetically given repository of such attributes that are commonly labeled thinking, problem solving, and speaking.

The way the mind works is the very subject matter of the cognitive image, and, on that account, is not necessarily contradictory in any way to the behavioral image. Behavior analysts can study verbal behavior and problem solving with a focus on how certain behavior is linked to certain environmental contingencies without being concerned with the nature of the behavioral repertoire that is the subject matter of study of a number of cognitive theorists. If the question arises as to the locus of control of the examined behavior, then behavior analysts part company with cognitive theorists.

The focus of practitioners of the historicosocial position are more similar to the cognitivists regarding the structure of mind than they are to the behavior analysts. However, locus of control is not an issue and thus the focus of the sociohistorical position is contradictory neither to the behavior analyst nor to the cognitive images. As we have seen, *verum-certum* (Vico) distinctions as well as the later distinction between *gemeinschaft* and *gesellshaft* are differences in the way human sensibility approaches the explanation of various phenomena around it. Language development in the individual and the social group is studied over historicosocial time. In conclusion, the structure of mind is (a) assumed to be part of the behavioral repertoire by the behavior analysts, (b) actively studied by cognitive theorists, and (c) actively studied by historicosocial theorists as part of group and individual developmental history.

Individual Behavior. Behavior analysts actively study the acquisition of individual organism behavior. In both the cognitive and historicosocial positions the acquisition of individual behavior is assumed and accepted without focus, as the structure of mind is accepted without focus by behavior analysts.

The laws of behavior acquisition as expressed, for example, in the schedules of reinforcement discussed earlier, are valid or not *on their own terms* for each of the three major positions. In short, nothing in the cognitive or historicosocial positions requires rejection of the laws of

FIG. 7.1. Characteristics of psychological images

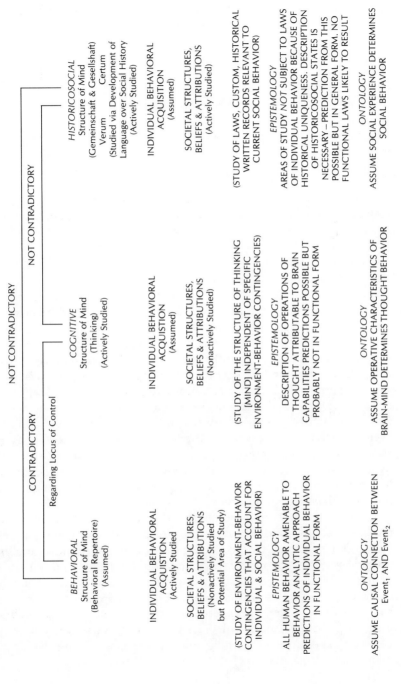

131

behavioral acquisition. They are simply assumed as of possible validity by the cognitive and historicosocial positions.

Societal Structures and Beliefs. The historicosocial approach is focused most upon the history and current structure of group laws, customs, and written records of social behavior. The historical development of language usage is also of critical interest. Cognitivists studying the structure of thinking (mind), independent of specific environmental contingencies, are not typically concerned with specific group history.

As behavior analysts are concerned with environment-behavior contingencies that they believe account for individual and social behavior, societal structures and beliefs have not been areas of great interest. Nor have they shown interest in the historical point of view regarding social activity.

Ontology and Epistemology. All three systems hedge when ontological questions are raised. Making ontological beliefs explicit subjects a theorist to declaring a position as of what his or her subject matter is fundamentally composed, and this is difficult for anyone who thinks of him or herself as a scientist. Nevertheless, all explanatory systems have functional ontologies usual implicit in the nature of the system. We have seen in chapter 5 that, although not stated, behavior analysts do make the tacit assumption that a causal connection exists as a relationship in nature when one pairs various reinforcements with specific behavior. The causal relationship is thus assumed to be an actual environmental relationship between that which is predicted and the event or event from which it is predicted. This implicit ontology is consistent with the espoused epistemological assumptions also made by the behavior analysts. It is assumed, explicitly, that all human behavior is amenable to prediction and therefore that the formation of functional laws is also possible.

The cognitive position assumes that the operative characteristics of the brain (called mind) determine the manner in which thought develops and is utilized. Consequently, the description of these thought operations is the appropriate way to understand the most complicated of human functions. It is rare that a cognitive theorist expects to be able to develop functional, predictive formulas in the manner of the behavior analyst. Rather, the expectation is that a general set of possibilities for human thought will be developed from which one may generate expectations regarding human problem solving, language usage, etc.

The unique assumption of the historicosocial position is that many behaviors called social cannot be reduced to the theoretical entities that we use to describe individual behavior. Rather, it is assumed that specific social experience generates social behavior. That is, human beings as much create the socius as they are formed by it. This, in turn, epistemologically requires that a description of historicosocial conditions is necessary to achieve an understanding of the possibilities for individual behavior of the members of the group. As is the case with cognitive theorists, it is not expected that functional, predictive laws will be developed from such description.

I hope I have convinced that the only major area of contradiction among the three positions or "images" is that regarding the locus of control of behavior, which is assumed to be either the environment (behavior analysts) or the capabilities of the organism (cognitive). On other important issues the three systems are focused on different questions, all concerning human beings but addressed to different phases of life.

Epilogue: The Limits and Possibilities of Explanation

Psychologists have never really had the luxury of simply calling themselves scientists, pure and simple, the way physicists, biologists, and chemists have had. We have wanted to be principally and only scientists as we studied ourselves and other animals, but there has always been at least one group of psychologists calling another "unscientific" or "soft-headed" since the days when Freud's efforts could be compared to those of Wundt's or Watson's. The problem has always been, whether we recognized it or not, that we have taken on what is perhaps the most difficult explanatory task ever. We purport to explain some of our own behavior, such as thinking and problem solving, by using those very behaviors in the process—a system doubling over on itself. As we all know, it has proved extremely difficult to accomplish enough to satisfy even our own expectations, much less those of the general public; particularly when we compare our efforts with those of the physicists or biologists. They don't have our problems. Physicists remain outside of the domain they attempt to explain in most important ways. The way that their own characteristics enter the domain of their explanatory process is largely trivial, even though it is true that a physicist, when dropped out of the window of a tall building, will fall at the rate of 32 feet per second per second. Psychologists, on the other hand, put themselves in a position of attempting to predict the behavior of a fellow human being while at the same time declaring their behavior is susceptible to similar predictions. As we know, this effort sometimes confuses us because it appears circular and self-contradictory. I hope I have shown that it is not contradictory or circular, if one acknowledges the different focal areas of the three major approaches to social behavior.

It also seems clear that, although the behavior analyst position successfully produces law-like statements, this is not possible for the cognitive and sociohistorical psychologists who depend heavily on description of existing states of mind or of society.

A question arises that is rarely raised in the psychological literature. Are there intrinsic limits to our ability to explain human behavior? If there are, are they different in kind than those technical limits that physics or biology, for example, suffer at any given point in their history and that have generally been overcome by some "break-through" in conception or equipment? If the division of effort that I have labeled behavioral, cognitive, and historicosocial is valid, then the indication at this point in the development of psychology is that there are intrinsic limitations to our ability to build successful theory and predict human behavior. This comment will undoubtedly provoke some into charging me with nihilism, skepticism, and defeatism. In addition, critics can cite the ignorance of more ancient times that was taken as immutable truth, such as the belief that the earth was the center of the universe, that human beings could not fly, and so on. I don't think these criticisms apply to my proposition, because most such examples show limitations in thinking about other than the human condition. To date there have been no real limitations in building explanations about the nonhuman universe. It is only when the constructors of these successful explanations turn their intelligence toward themselves that problems arise. This book has attempted to catalog such problems without being nihilistic, skeptical, or defeatist.

What I have attempted to show is that for at least 300 years since the time of Descartes, reasonably sophisticated arguments as to the nature of human existence have been built that continued to be active in some more useful fashion down to the present. Undoubtedly, elements of these arguments can be found for 1,600 years prior to Descartes as well. Psychological explanation has progressed mightily since Descartes, and what is most impressive to me is that we understand better today than we did in the past how explanations of human existence change in their ontological and epistemological qualities as the questions we ask shift our focus from one area to another. I hope I have been able to indicate how this happens.

Thinking about thinking, solving the problems of problem solving, and speaking about language development may represent limits to human understanding of the way human beings work. In contrast, our understanding of brain function has progressed significantly and will most likely continue to progress for a long time.

These limits are reflected in what many psychologists see as the breakdown of behavioral, noncognitive systems in explaining the higher mental processes, and the shift from specific predictions to description in cognitive theories when they address themselves to the same subject matter.

In social psychology, as we have seen (Marcus & Zajonc, 1985), much current research has shifted emphasis from the predictive experiment to the careful description of social context where expectations of human social response replace the quantified prediction.

What approach is used depends on what answer one seeks to what question. The focus of the theorist is crucial and should be explicit.

References

Abelson, R. P. (1976). Script processing in attitude formation and decision making. In J. S. Carroll & J. W. Payne (Eds.), *Cognition and social behavior* (pp. 33–45). Hillsdale, NJ: Lawrence Erlbaum Associates.

Adler, M. J. (1927). *Dialectic.* New York: Harcourt Brace.

Altman, I. (1976). Environmental psychology and social psychology. *Personality and Social Psychology Bulletin, 2,* 96–113.

Anderson, N. H. (1962). Information integration theory: A brief survey. In D. H. Krantz, R. C. Atkinson, R. D. Luce, & P. Suppes (Eds.), *Contemporary developments in mathematical psychology* (Vol. 2). New York: Freeman.

Anderson, N. H. (1981). *Foundations of information integration theory.* New York: Academic Press.

Anscombe, G. E. M. (1957). *Intention.* Oxford: Basil Blackwell.

Aronson, E., & Bridgeman, P. (1979). Jigsaw groups and the desegregated classroom: In pursuit of common goals. *Personality and Social Psychology Bulletin, 5,* 438–446.

Asch, S. E. (1946). Studies of independence and conformity. I. A minority of one against a unanimous majority. *Psychological Monographs, 70* (9, Whole No. 416).

Billig, M. (1987). *Arguing and thinking—A rhetorical approach to social psychology.* London: Cambridge University Press.

Braithwaite, R. B. (1960). *Scientific explanation.* New York: Harper.

Brentano, F. (1973). *Psychology from an empirical standpoint* (A. C. Rancurello, D. B. Terrell, & L. L. McAlister, Trans.). London: Routledge Kegan Paul.

Bruner, J. S. (1951). Personality dynamics and the process of perceiving. In R. R. Blake & G. V. Ramsey (Eds.), *Perception: An approach to personality* (pp. 121–147). New York: Ronald.

Bunge, M. (1959). *Causality.* Cambridge, MA: Harvard University Press.

Buss, A. R. (1978). Causes and reasons in attribution theory: A conceptual critique. *Journal of Personality and Social Psychology, 36,* 1311–1321.

Cantor, N. (1979). Prototypicality and personality: Effects on free recall and personality impressions. *Journal of Research in Personality, 13,* 187–205.

Cantor, N., & Mischel, W. (1977). Traits as prototypes: Effects on recognition memory. *Journal of Personality and Social Psychology, 35,* 38–48.

Chein, I. (1972). *The science of behavior and the image of man.* New York: Basic Books.

Chisholm, R. M. (1957). *Perceiving: A philosophical study.* New York: Cornell University Press.

Chomsky, N. (1964). *Current issues in linguistic theory.* The Hague: Mouton.

Chomsky, N. (1966). *Cartesian linguistics: A chapter in the history of rationalist thought.* New York: Harper & Row.

Cioffi, F. (1982, April). *Comments on human studies and the empirical sciences.* Speech presented at the Philadelphia Philosophy Consortium, Bryn Mawr College, Bryn Mawr, PA.

Day, W. F. (1969). Radical behaviorism in reconciliation with phenomenology. *Journal of the Experimental Analysis of Behavior, 12,* 315–328.

Day, W. F. (1976). Contemporary behaviorism and the concept of intention. In W. J. Arnold (Ed.), *Nebraska symposium on motivation, 1975* (pp. 65–131). Lincoln, NE: University of Nebraska Press.

Descartes, Spinoza, Leibniz: (No date) *The rationalists.* Garden City, NY: Doubleday Dolphin.

Dilthey, W. (1977). *Descriptive psychology and historical understanding.* (R. M. Zaner & K. L. Heiges, Trans.). The Hague: Nijhoff.

Doise, W. (1986). *Levels of explanation in social psychology.* London: Cambridge University Press.

Dollard, J., & Miller, N. (1950). *Personality and psychotherapy.* New York: McGraw-Hill.

Epstein, S. (1973). The self-concept revisited: Or a theory of a theory. *American Psychologist, 28,* 404–416.

Ferster, C. B., & Skinner, B. F. (1957). *Schedules of reinforcement.* New York: Appleton-Century-Crofts.

Fishbein, M., & Ajzen, I. (1972). Attitudes and opinions. In P. H. Mussen & M. R. Rosensweig (Eds.), *Annual review of psychology* (Vol. 23, pp. 487–544). Palo Alto, CA: Annual Reviews.

Follesdal, D. (1981, October). *Comments on intentionality and rationality.* Speech presented at the Philadelphia Philosophy Consortium at Bryn Mawr College, Bryn Mawr, PA.

Friedman, M. (1967). *To deny our nothingness: Contemporary images of man.* New York: Delta.

Freud, S. (1960). *The ego and the id* (J. Riviere & J. Strachey, Trans.). New York: Norton.

Gadamer, H. (1975). *Truth and method.* New York: Seabury.

Gergen, K. (1973). Social psychology as history. *Journal of Personality and Social Psychology, 26,* 309–320.

Habermas, J. (1971). *Knowledge and human interests.* Boston: Beacon Press.

Hinline, P. N. (1990). The origins of environment-based psychological theory. *Journal of the Experimental Analysis of Behavior, 53,* 305–320.

Hineline, P. N., & Wanchisen, B. A. (1989). Correlated hypothesizing, and the distinction between contingency-shaped and rule-governed behavior. In S. C. Hayes (Ed.), *Rule-governed behavior: Cognition, contingencies, and instructional control* (pp. 221–268). New York: Plenum.

Hobbes, T. (1904). *Leviathan.* Cambridge, England: University Press (Original work published 1651)

Hovland, C. I., Janis, I. L., & Kelley, H. H. (1953). *Communication and persuasion.* New Haven: Yale University Press.

Hovland, C. I., Lumsdaine, A. A., & Sheffield, F. D. (1949). *Experiments on mass persuasion.* Princeton: Princeton University Press.

Hull, C. L. (1943). *Principles of behavior.* New York: Appleton-Century-Crofts.

Hull, C. L. (1952). *A behavior system.* New Haven: Yale University Press.

Hume, D. (1961). *A treatise of human nature.* Garden City, NY: Doubleday-Dolphin.

Husserl, E. (1960). *Cartesian mediation: An introduction to phenomenology.* The Hague: Nijhoff.

Husserl, E. (1964). *The idea of phenomenology.* The Hague: Nijhoff.

James, W. (1962). *Psychology* (briefer course). New York: Collier Books.

Johnson, J. (1989). On the implications of the relativity/quantum revolution for psychology. In D. A. Kramer & M. J. Bopp (Eds.), *Transformation in clinical and developmental psychology* (pp. 25–50). New York: Springer-Verlag.

Jones, E. E., & Nisbett, R. E. (1971). *The actor and the observer: Divergent perceptions of the causes of behavior.* Morristown, NJ: General Learning Press.

Jones, E. E., & Thibault, J. W. (1958). Interaction goals as bases of inference in interpersonal perception. In R. Tagiuri & K. Petrullo (Eds.), *Person perception and interpersonal behavior* (pp. 151–178). Stanford: Stanford University Press.

Kant, I. (1961). *Critique of pure reason.* New York: Doubleday-Dolphin.

Kelley, H. H. (1973). The process of causal attribution. *American Psychologist, 28,* 107–128.

Kohler, W. (1959). Gestalt psychology today. *American Psychologist, 14,* 727–734.

Kuhn, T. S. (1970). *The structure of scientific revolutions* (2nd ed.). Chicago: University of Chicago Press.

Lana, R. E. (1969). *Assumptions of social psychology.* New York: Appleton-Century-Crofts.

Lana, R. E. (1976). *The foundations of psychological theory.* Hillsdale, NJ: Lawrence Erlbaum Associates.

Lana, R. E. (1986). Descartes, Vico, contextualism and social psychology. In R. Rosnow & M. Georgoudi (Eds.), *Contextualism and understanding in behavioral science* (pp. 67–85). New York: Praeger.

Lana, R. E., & Georgoudi, M. (1983). Causal attributions: Phenomenological and dialectical aspects. *Journal of Mind and Behavior, 4,* 479–490.

Lashley, K. S. (1923). The behavioristic interpretation of consciousness II. *Psychological Review, 30,* 329–353.

Lauer, Q. (1958). *Phenomenology: Its genesis and prospect.* New York: Harper Torchbooks.

Lerner, J. M. (1975). Locus of control, perceived responsibility for prior fate. *Journal of Research in Personality, 9,* 1–20.

Lindzey, G., & Aronson, E. (1985). *The handbook of social psychology* (Vols. I and II, 3rd ed.). New York: Random House.

Lingle, J. H., & Ostrom, T. M. (1979). Retrieval selectivity on memory-based judgements. *Journal of Personality and Social Psychology, 37,* 180–194.

Locke, J. (1690). *Essay concerning human understanding.* London: Basset.

Mach, E, (1959). *The analysis of sensation.* New York: Dover.

Markus, H., & Zajonc, R. B. (1985). The cognitive perspective in social psychology. In G. Lindzey & E. Aronson (Eds.), *The handbook of social psychology* (pp. 137–230). New York: Random House.

May, R. (1961). *Existential psychology.* New York: Random House.

McGuire, W. (1985). Attitudes and attitude change. In G. Lindzey & E. Aronson (Eds.), *The handbook of social psychology* (pp. 233–346). New York: Random House.

Merleau-Ponty, M. (1962) *Phenomenology of perception.* New York: Humanities Press.

Merleau-Ponty, M. (1963). *The structure of behavior.* Boston: Beacon.

Minsky, M. (1975). A framework for representing knowledge. In P. H. Winston (Ed.), *The psychology of computer vision.* New York: McGraw-Hill.

Mooney, M. (1985). *Vico in the tradition of rhetoric.* Princeton: Princeton University Press.

Morawski, J. G. (1986). Contextual discipline: The unmaking and remaking of sociality. In R. L. Rosnow & M. Georgoudi (Eds.), *Contextualism and understanding in behavioral science* (pp. 47–66). New York: Praeger.

Neisser, U. (1976). *Cognition and reality: Principles and implications of cognitive psychology.* San Francisco: Freeman.

Nietzsche, F. (1966). *Beyond good and evil.* New York: Doubleday Anchor.

Nisbett, R. E., & Ross, L. (1980). *Human inference: Strategies and shortcomings in social judgement.* Englewood Cliffs, NJ: Prentice-Hall.

Ricoeur, P. (1981). Hermeneutics and the human sciences. In J. B. Thompson (Ed.), *Essays in language, action and interpretation.* Cambridge: Cambridge University Press.

Ringen, J. (1976). Explanation, teleology, and operant behaviorism: A study of the experimental basis of purposive behavior. *Philosophy of Science, 43,* 223–253.

Robinson, J. K., & Woodward, W. R. (1989). The convergence of behavioral biology and operant psychology: Toward an interlevel and interfield science. *The Behavior Analyst, 12,* 131–141.

Rosch, E. H. (1973). Natural categories. *Cognitive psychology, 4,* 328–350.

Rosenthal, R., & Rosnow, R. L. (1969). *Artifact in behavioral research.* New York: Academic Press.

Rosnow, R. L. (1981). *Paradigms in transition: The methodology of social inquiry.* New York: Oxford University Press.

Rosnow, R. L., & Georgoudi, M. (Eds.). (1986). *Contextualism and understanding in behavioral science.* New York: Praeger.

Russell, B. (1960). *Our knowledge of the external world.* New York: The New American Library.

Russell, B. (1962). *Human knowledge, its scope and limits.* New York: Simon & Schuster.

Ryan, T. A. (1970). *Intentional behavior: An approach to human motivation.* New York: Ronald Press.

Rychlak, J. F. (1987). Can the strength of past associations account for the direction of thought? *Journal of Mind and Behavior, 8,* 185–194.

Skinner, B. F. (1953). *Science and human behavior.* New York: Macmillan.

Skinner, B. F. (1957). *Verbal behavior.* New York: Appleton-Century-Crofts.

Skinner, B. F. (1976). *About behaviorism.* New York: Vintage Books.

Slife, B. D. (1987). Can cognitive psychology account for metacognitive functions of mind? *Journal of Mind and Behavior, 8,* 195–208.

Smith, E. E., & Medin, D. L. (1981). *Categories and concepts.* Cambridge, MA: Harvard University Press.

Spence, K. (1956). *Behavior theory and conditioning.* New Haven: Yale University Press.

Stotland, E., & Cannon, L. K. (1972). *Social psychology: A cognitive approach.* Philadelphia: Saunders.

Tesser, A., & Cowan, C. L. (1975). Some effects of thought and number of cognitions on attitude change. *Social Behavior and Personality, 3,* 165–173.

Tesser, A., & Cowan, C. L. (1977). Some attitudinal and cognitive consequences of thought. *Journal of Research in Personality, 11,* 216–226.

Tolman, E. C. (1927). A behaviorist's definition of consciousness. *Psychological Review, 34,* 433–439.

Tooley, M. (1987). *Causation.* Oxford: Clarendon Press.

Vico, G. (1961). *The new science of Giambattista Vico.* Garden City, NY: Doubleday-Anchor.

Vico, G. (1988). *On the most ancient wisdom of the Italians* (L. M. Palmer, Trans.). Ithaca, NY: Cornell University Press.

Walster, E. (1966). Assignment of responsibility for an accident. *Journal of Personality and Social Psychology, 3,* 73–79.

Watson, J. B. (1913). Psychology as the behaviorist views it. *Psychological Review, 20,* 158–177.

Watson, J. D. (1968). *The double helix.* New York: Atheneum.

Wiener, N. (1948). *Cybernetics: Control and communication in the animal and the machine.* Cambridge, MA: Technology Press.

Winch, P. (1958). *The idea of a social science.* New York: Humanities Press.

Wortman, C. B. (1976). Causal attributions and personal control. In J. H. Harvey, W. J. Ickes, & R. F. Kidd (Eds.), *New directions in attribution research* (Vol. 1, pp. 23–52). Hillsdale, NJ: Lawrence Erlbaum Associates.

Author Index

Subject Index